CDL MINDED ENTREPRENEUR

3-STEP SYSTEM TO LEVERAGE TIME,

HAVE UNLIMITED FREEDOM AND MAXIMIZE SECURITY IN THE CDL INDUSTRY

JOE RYDER

Interior design by FormattedBooks

Table of Contents

STEP 2: CDL-Minded in YOUR 'Business'

STEP 3: Living the CDL-Minded Lifestyle

Special Bonus Offer: Free Gift for You! :)

CDL Business Productivity GAME PLAN

Entrepreneurs Guide to Quick Start your Business to the Next Level

Thank you! Here's a Free Gift! For You :)

As a special thanks from me to you, you'll receive:

- ❏ **3 Powerful Elements of Productivity in your Business**
- ❏ **5 Simple Strategies to Mastering Productivity in your Business**
- ❏ **The Highest Quality of Productivity Charts**
- ❏ **Valuable Resources that you Must Know and much more!**

To receive your Free copy of the CDL Business Productivity GAME PLAN, you can go to my website at:
cdlforlife.com/cdl-business-resources

SCAN ME
(For your Free Business Game Plan)

SCAN ME
(If you want my Books for Free)

Also If you would like to get my books for Free and before anyone else, go to my website at:
cdlforlife.com/cdl-business-resources

Introduction

Before becoming an entrepreneur in the CDL industry, work was just something I did to pay the bills. Coming home on the verge of exhaustion used to be just another day for me. I would walk in the front door with hardly enough energy to stumble over to the couch, as the aches and pains of the day and my long schedule caught up with me. I barely had the energy to watch half an episode of TV before I fell asleep halfway from the couch to the bedroom, let alone having enough energy to spend quality time with my family. I was working myself to the bone, all for wages that only barely covered all of my expenses. The worst part of it all was that I knew I would just have to do it all again the next day. It seemed like there was no end in sight.

This is probably a familiar story to many of you. Work can dominate your life, even and especially if you're not making enough money to be able to save some. If your job is routine, menial work, it becomes even harder to dedicate so much of your life to it. This is the life that so many people lead, but that doesn't mean it's the only option. After living this way for years, I decided that it wasn't how I wanted to live the rest of my life. I didn't want work to take up such a large portion of my day that I didn't have any time for my family. I didn't want to be so tired that my hobbies and passions fell by the wayside. I didn't want to struggle with my finances, trying to decide whether or not I could afford a new pair of shoes this week, or if I had to wait until my next payday. I was tired of being tired, and I knew if I wanted my life to change, it had to start with my job.

Becoming an entrepreneur in the Commercial Driver's License (CDL) and commercial trucking industry was my ticket out. When I made the decision to become a CDL entrepreneur, so many things in my life changed. I set my own hours and had more time away from work so that I could spend time with my family more often. As my business grew bigger and more successful, I had more money, so I wasn't always worrying about financial troubles. I found that commercial trucking was my passion, and I felt more fulfilled doing work I really cared about. I found I had more control over my life, and that sense of control helped me feel more content with my life as a whole. My life was entirely changed by this decision, and yours can change too.

You can have a job that you really care about and that you excel in. You can be your own boss, choose when you want to work and when you want to take time off, and experience more freedom both in the workplace and in your personal life. You can live on a comfortable income, and free yourself from the constant stress that money-trouble creates. When you become an entrepreneur in the CDL industry, you get to call the shots and regain control over your life.

Building your own business is never an easy process, and the CDL industry is no exception. However, if you develop the right mindset and become "CDL-Minded," you can practically guarantee future success. When you start thinking like an entrepreneur, it becomes easy to expand your company into a profitable business. With CDL-Minded Entrepreneur, you will learn how to make smart and wise business decisions in a lucrative marketplace. I will help you devise a plan for establishing and developing your company. I will also walk you through the process of developing the mindset you need in order to make your CDL business a success so that you can enjoy personal and financial freedom.

Driving and operating a truck driving business is a labor of love for me. It is an industry that is so important to me, and one that I genuinely love working in. I know the ins and outs of the commercial driving business because it has been a part of my life for over 25 years. I have been a commercial operator, business entrepreneur, truck driver, and instructor to many students. I operated my own multi-million dol-lar business, and I have taught my students how they can achieve the same level of success. This is life-changing information, as my students have gone on to earn at least $60,000 to $100,000 a year with their own businesses. They have told me that they cannot imagine starting and maintaining a business without the critical guidance I have provided, especially the three-step system, which you too will learn.

What you're about to discover has been a closely guarded secret kept by many Fortune 500 companies. The CDL trucking industry will never tell you these secrets, but I will unveil the way you can drastically increase your profits and your chances of long-term, lasting success. I will take you, step-by-step, through the process of creating and sustaining a truly profitable company. I believe that everyone, not just the wealthy elite, should have the opportunity to reach this level of success, and I want to help you achieve it. By following my strategies, you could make enough money to retire in as little as five years, secure in the knowledge that you'll never need to work another day in your life if you don't want to. You will be able to live far beyond your current financial means. Rather than being trapped by the daily grind at work, you will experience unlimited freedom in your new life as an entrepreneur in the commercial trucking industry.

It's time for you to make the same change in your life that I made in mine. It's time to start your own company in the CDL industry and enjoy all of the wealth and freedom that comes with it. You will face some challenges, but if you are really committed to improving your quality of life, you won't let that hold you back. When you start thinking about the road ahead as an exciting new opportunity, you'll soon find that all of the challenges were worth the amazing results. If you want to run a successful business that ensures you'll never have to miss out on family time or worry about your financial situation again, you need to become a CDL-Minded Entrepreneur.

STEP 1

CDL-Minded Starts With YOURSELF

CHAPTER 1

Making the Decision and Applying the CDL-Minded Habits

Becoming a CDL entrepreneur is much more than a simple career change. If you really want to be an effective CDL business owner, you must step out of the mindset of the typical employee. No matter what your previous job was, owning your own business is a big step. It's going to require you to turn your thinking around and really embrace the idea of thinking like an entrepreneur. This will also require you to adopt CDL-Minded habits to ensure your success. But what does a CDL-Minded approach really mean?

Being CDL-Minded means more than just taking on additional responsibilities. It means thinking, feeling, and acting like you're a professional in the CDL industry. If you want to make it big, you'll want to go in with a mindset that promotes success. You need to believe that you will be successful before you even take your first few steps. Having a confident, forward-thinking mindset will give you the passion you need to start this new life journey, and the tenacity you need to see it through even when times get tough. It is not enough to just work like an entrepreneur; you must think and live like an entrepreneur.

This change in your mindset doesn't happen overnight. It takes dedication to start thinking this way, especially if you are used to working for others and just putting in the required effort to get your job done. You're going to have to start actively seeking out opportunities and rethinking the way you approach your job. Changing your mindset also requires clarity on your goals and dreams. This begins with some self-discovery so you can understand just what your life's purpose is and why it matters to you. This process influences your mission statement and vision for the future. It will also help you start adopting healthy, ambition-driven habits that allow you to set and achieve your goals. When you understand what you want, and you spend time training yourself into the mindset of a successful entrepreneur, it becomes much more likely that you will actually become a successful entrepreneur in the CDL industry.

Finding Your Life's Purpose

Our life's purpose is the reason why we're here on this earth. Finding our purpose gives our very existence meaning. It is what we should strive to accomplish every day. Without knowing our purpose, we might wander around blindly through life, moving from job to job, toiling away under someone else's thumb for years. We could waste our precious time doing a job we hate that isn't suitable for our lifestyle. If we want to feel fulfilled in life, we must find and pursue our life's purpose.

Of course, this information isn't easy to come by. Many people go their whole lives without finding something they're passionate about. In order to understand your life's purpose, you need to take some time to really think about what your ideal life would look like. It requires a lot of self-reflection and visualization. Are you relaxing on a beach, enjoying personal comforts, and no longer stressing out over financial concerns? Do you have a big, loving family with plenty of kids and grandkids? Do you volunteer or otherwise support people in your community? Do you wake up in the morning each day excited for your job, and if so, what job is it?

Answering these kinds of questions by visualizing your ideal future can help you understand the value of your life and how you can achieve self-fulfillment. In order to arrive at these answers, you must have a deep understanding of yourself, your needs, and your desires. It is only then that you can start to effectively pursue your goals.

The Importance of Knowing Your Purpose

What happens if we go through life without a purpose? Would it really be so bad? As previously mentioned, it's not something that everyone realizes during their lives. Surely, you might think we could live without taking all this time for self-reflection. We very well might be able to live, but simply living is different from thriving. We can go through the motions, but feelings of self-fulfillment will continue to elude us.

Rather than being fully present each day, we go on a sort of autopilot through life. Our days are made up of the same dull routine, and we continue going through the motions without really taking note of what we are doing. We know that there's more to life than this, but we don't really feel the need to achieve anything else, or if we do, it's only for the sake of making ourselves more comfortable. Most people shy away from opportunities that require them to work a bit harder for a bigger reward because they don't see them as being steps to a better life. They lack the ambition required to do something really daring and different, which means they just do the work others tell them to do. This kind of mindset can keep us from venturing out into becoming an entrepreneur.

When we take time to discover and understand our life's purpose, we also discover a reason to leave our previous lives behind and aim for a better quality of life. We find a drive and motivation that encourages us to get up and get moving. This makes it possible for us to take the daring and often scary leap into becoming an entrepreneur. There will be a lot of uncertainty, but if we are working towards our life's purpose, we won't let that stop us. In fact, there's very little that will stop us when we find the proper motivation in life.

No one ever became successful by living a completely unchallenged life. It is impossible to go through life without facing challenges, whether they appear in our careers or our personal lives. When we encounter these challenges, we have two options. We can let valuable opportunities pass us by and decide that the trouble is not worth the reward, shrug, and back down from the challenge. If we choose this path, we'll never make any progress towards our goals.

On the other hand, we can look at these challenges as chances to better ourselves and get closer to what we want. When we start seeing them as stepping stones leading towards our long-term goals, it is much easier to take them on, not just begrudgingly, but with genuine passion and feeling. We can see how each challenge fits into the bigger picture, and the desire to avoid difficulties in life starts to fade away as we plan for bigger and better things.

Being a CDL entrepreneur means facing plenty of challenges each day. It means trying to build a new company from the ground up. It means learning new skills necessary for running a business, such as accounting, people skills, and having a good nose for business. If you previously worked in a different industry, it might even mean learning all about the CDL industry and the ways that you can make your company stand out and find success. However, if all of these challenges are standing in the way of achieving your life's goals, they won't be such big roadblocks after all. You'll find yourself ready and even eager to take them on, as doing so brings you closer to what you really want in life. You will find yourself freed from the chains of uncertainty and living on autopilot, ready to keep moving in life no matter what comes next. So long as you can find the motivation to keep going, it is only a matter of time before you achieve personal and professional success in the CDL industry and in your life as a whole.

How to Identify and Apply Your Life's Purpose

Even after you know how important having a purpose is, it can still be hard to identify the unique goals and interests that appeal to you. When you try to picture your ideal future, your mind might draw a blank. There are so many possible paths our lives can take, with many different outcomes. How do we even begin deciding on the outcome we want to achieve, and once we do, how do we get there?

If you're stumped, try narrowing your scope a bit. Rather than trying to decide what you want your entire future to look like, focus on more specific details like your financial situation and your family. First, identify the parts of your life that bring you dissatisfaction. Look for areas where you feel unfulfilled or times when you felt exhausted and worn down. Next, think about how you could improve upon these areas. From there, you can get a better picture of what matters to you and how you can start working to achieve these goals. Ideally, you also want to begin considering how becoming an entrepreneur in the CDL industry can help you reach your full potential.

Even with this narrowed focus, looking to the future can be tough. It helps to break down your goals into three different areas: what you want for yourself, what you want for your family, and what you want for your community group or culture.

Start with the things you want for yourself in your life. Think about what you'd like to achieve in areas such as your dream job, your ideal financial situation, and your current or future family. If you could lead any life you wanted to, what would it be? Do you want a fast-paced job, where every day presents you with a new challenge you get to solve, or would you rather have a slow, relaxed life that is more focused on your personal relationships than your career? Are you looking to build up a nice financial cushion to coast on comfortably, or are you interested in becoming truly wealthy? Do you want a big family with kids, or do you not have any immediate plans for expanding your current family? Identifying what *you* want should come first before you worry about what others may want from you.

Once you know what your own personal goals are, you can consider if your current lifestyle is helping you achieve these goals, or if you need to make some changes. You should also take a moment to consider how becoming a CDL entrepreneur ties back into these personal goals. If you want to start living comfortably, but you always find yourself facing money troubles, starting your own CDL business can help you increase your income. If you want to be able to spend more time with your kids, running your own business can provide you with the freedom to choose your own hours. This gives you more free time to share with your family.

Consider personal goals that involve developing and cultivating certain personal values as well. You might want to build greater self-confidence, work on your charisma, improve your interpersonal skills, or refine any number of areas where you feel you have limited experience. Making improvements to these kinds of skills can help you become a more well-rounded person while also supporting your pursuit of your other goals. Becoming a CDL entrepreneur can help with developing these skills too.

As you start taking charge in your own company, you will become better at managing conflicts and thinking critically about a problem to arrive at an effective solution. Inspiring confidence in your business means acting confidently yourself, and the more experience you get putting yourself into uncertain situations, the easier it becomes to accept that risk is just a part of success. Taking note of how the experiences you will gain as a CDL entrepreneur can contribute to all of your personal goals, will help you remain motivated throughout the process of establishing and running your own company.

Next, consider your life's purpose in terms of your family. What do you want for your family? What kinds of lives do you want to help your kids lead? This is a little different than thinking about what you want your family to look like. Instead, you should consider what kind of goals you can achieve together and how you can set them up for success. Maybe you want to save enough money so your children's college expenses are covered. Maybe you want your kids to come work with you in your future CDL business when they're old enough, or you want to show them the value of hard work in life no matter what their dreams are. You might also have goals related to things you and your spouse can achieve together, like good communication and caring deeply about each other, or perhaps working together in this new entrepreneurial venture in your life.

Finally, think about how your life's purpose relates to your community and culture. How can you improve the lives of those around you? Why does it matter to you that your community is improved? Think about the charitable causes that matter most to you, which are often those that have had a direct impact on your life. Some people get involved in fundraising for cancer research centers because they have lost a relative to cancer. Others work to support their local food banks because they know what it is like to go hungry.

Once you've identified a positive change you can make in your community, consider how you can best support these efforts. Sometimes this means volunteering to help out at a fundraising or awareness-raising event. Other times it might mean donating some money or goods where they are needed most. While there are countless ways you can get involved right now, becoming a CDL entrepreneur can help you make an even bigger impact. It can give you the flexible schedule and free time you need to be able to volunteer, or the extra savings that you can donate to help others. By improving your own life, you can improve the lives of many others.

Charity work isn't the only way you can support your community. You might find that pursuing a hobby with your newfound free time and developing your skills in a creative pursuit, like art or writing, can help too. Even just reaching out and talking to others in your community, trying to foster a genuine connection, can help you make a positive impact on your neighbors. Doing some good in the world, no matter how you choose to do it, can help you feel like you are living a more fulfilling life and show you the value of your efforts in improving the lives of others.

Overall Mindset Approach

Our life's purpose should inform and influence our overall mindset. When we know what we want to do with our lives, it becomes much easier to convince ourselves that we are capable of doing it. Focusing on our goals gives us a positive mindset that encourages us to take action and work towards the results we want to see. Setting specific goals and understanding how our choices make an impact on our ability to achieve these goals is imperative. Our desire to achieve our long-term goals gives us the strength we need to leave our current jobs behind and pursue becoming a CDL entrepreneur.

If we don't set goals in line with our purpose in life, we can have trouble shaking ourselves out of our daily routine, even if the current routine is unfulfilling. We might continue living our lives aimlessly, just taking one day at a time and never seeing how valuable each day can be for getting closer to our goals. When we set goals, we subconsciously remind ourselves that we are capable of improving the things that bring us dissatisfaction in life. Our lives become a pathway towards our goals, which makes us more likely to take a risk or make a big career change.

Breaking our goals down into individual, family, and community goals demonstrate how each type of goal feeds into the next. The goals we set at an individual level are instrumental in achieving our family-oriented goals, which in turn help us achieve our community goals. Saving money for our children's education is only possible if we achieve the financial freedom we desire. We can only donate any excess money to charitable causes we are passionate about if we have first made sure our families are well taken care of. If we want to help our communities, we must first help ourselves. Achieving our individual goals gives us both the ability and the drive to achieve other life goals.

Setting short-term and long-term goals is key for success. We need to adopt a goal-oriented mindset if we want to fulfill our purpose in life. Keeping our goals in mind helps us make decisions that bring us closer to success and fulfillment. It also helps keep us motivated when we face difficult challenges. When striking out as an entrepreneur, you will face plenty of difficulties, whether they come in the form of learning how to build a company from scratch, managing employees, dealing with finances, or any number of other possible issues. However, when you are focused on achieving your goals, it becomes much easier to take these challenges in stride. If you care about the product of your work, it hardly feels like work at all.

Mission and Vision Statements

Part of understanding your purpose is understanding your vision for the future and your mission statement, both as an individual and for your future company. Your mission and vision statements should be a representation of who you are, what you stand for, and what you work to achieve as a whole. It should reflect what matters most to you and guides your actions.

If your vision for yourself is to be more optimistic and always look for silver linings on dark clouds, you should try to reexamine negative and self-defeating thoughts when they appear. If your vision for your company is to provide top-quality service, the way your company functions should prioritize giving customers this high-quality experience. In other words, your mission statement is the way that you provide unique value to yourself, your family, your community, and to the marketplace. It is what helps you stand out from the crowd and build a more personal relationship with your community and your customers alike.

Developing a clear idea of your mission statement will help you keep your focus on the future. It will also help you make tough choices where you need to prioritize one service at the expense of another. Ideally, you'd want your company to provide a service that is quick, high-quality, and low-cost, but sometimes this just isn't possible, especially when you are just starting out. You might need to sacrifice a bit of quality in order to get things moving faster, or you might need to charge more if you're focusing on providing the best possible service. If you know your company's mission statement, you can make a choice that matches your priorities. Many companies can charge more for a speedy premium service, while others do their business by being quick and cheap, even if the end results are a little rushed. Think of a business like Walmart, which is known for having slightly lower quality products but which offers some of the lowest possible prices. Alternatively, customers who care more about quality are likely to shop at more specialty stores, but at a greater cost for most products. The differences between a big-box retailer like Walmart and a specialty boutique come from differences in their mission statements.

What you choose to prioritize in your own company will depend on what kind of service you want to provide. A mission statement that promises customers speedy service first and foremost should prioritize that above all else; the same is true of companies that promise quality or low prices. The decisions you make as you begin to establish your CDL company and the actions you take now to expand your business will be a product of your mission statement and your vision for the future of your company.

How to Apply Your Mission and Vision Statements

Applying your mission and vision statements is a similar process to applying your life's purpose. They both help guide your decisions and give you the motivation to pursue your long-term goals. Just like you did with your life's purpose, you can break down your mission statement into your individual vision, your vision for your family, and your vision for your community or culture group.

Write out your individual vision or personal mission statement first. It is a representation of who you are as a person and what you want to accomplish. It should include both your purpose and how you want to achieve that purpose. Try to include your skills, your personality traits, and the dreams and passions that you want to pursue. For example, maybe you highly value helping others reach their goals. Your mission statement might say that you want to be a teacher for others and that you want to show them how they can be successful and encourage their growth. You might value giving each client the best possible service and a personal yet professional experience. Your mission statement can be something like trying to always learn more every day and growing as a person, or trying to be someone your friends and family can rely on in a crisis.

Once you've identified your personal vision, take steps to fulfill your promise to yourself. Teaching others means finding your own success first, then sharing that knowledge as a mentor figure.

Prioritizing amazing service might mean you have to work a little harder than your peers, but if you're really committed to providing the best service for customers, the extra work will be worth it. Being reliable means helping others out even when it inconveniences you. You may need to make sacrifices or tough decisions in many of these examples, but you will feel more personally fulfilled if you stick to your individual mission statement.

Next, write out your mission statement for your family. What should your family value most above all other things? What standards should you keep for how you interact with each other and how you behave towards others? Maybe you want your family to be loving and supportive of each other. Maybe you want to share a lot of quality time and really come together. Having a family mission statement can help your family push back against some common but potentially harmful societal trends. Therefore, creating your own culture of caring for each other is one of the most healthy ways to keep a family together. Focusing on family bonding is another way to keep kids out of trouble and even deepen the relationship between yourself and your significant other.

Your family culture should take into account the goals of all of your family members. When in doubt, talk to your family and ask them what they feel is missing. Do your kids feel like you are a present parent, or is too much of your time spent at work? Do they feel like they can talk to you about their struggles? Though it may not initially seem like it, becoming an entrepreneur can help you live along the guidelines established by your family mission statement. For example, having more control over your schedule can help you spend more time with everyone. With a little more money in your savings, you could go on that family vacation you've been putting off. The simple act of allocating more time for your family can show them you really care and help you all grow closer.

Finally, write your mission statement for your culture or community. What kind of service do you want to provide to your community, and why does providing that service matter to you? It is easy to get wrapped up in caring about ourselves, but when we expand our focus and care about the well-being of others, we often feel better about ourselves in return. A mission statement that prioritizes your community might involve a dedication to community service, or a desire to operate in a way that supports your area by hiring locally and making sure your employees are being treated fairly.

These kinds of goals can be achieved by making donations with a company or personal profits or volunteering your time. You might also choose to be very vocal about issues that matter to you in order to raise awareness. Having a successful business can help with this too—when celebrities and successful entrepreneurs speak out on issues, their large audience turns the issue into a talking point, which can lead to more donations or public support. These kinds of actions often have the added benefit of more public support for your business, too, as people come to see you as a charitable company.

Overall Mindset Approach

Your personal mission statement and the mission statement you create for your business should work in tandem to help you accomplish your goals. They should both influence your overall mindset and keep you striving for positive change at all times. Vision statements give you purpose and direction. They help you choose a course and stick to that course, and they guide you through otherwise tough decisions. Trying to achieve your vision statement with every decision you make with your business trains your brain to prioritize the things that will get you closer to your long-term goals.

Your vision statement should also influence the working environment of your business. When you first start out, you will probably only have a handful of people working for your business, but as you continue to grow, you will have many employees. If you maintain a clear mission statement and make sure that your employees are aware of your company mission, they are more likely to share the same values in their work. If employees get the sense that their company doesn't care about the quality of their work, they won't care about it either. On the other hand, a company that prioritizes quality work will train its employees to prioritize quality work too. Mission and vision statements are critical to fostering a positive and productive mindset for both yourself and your employees.

Long-Term Health

If you want to be successful, you need to get and stay healthy. Poor health habits jeopardize your chances of reaching your goals. A health scare could mean you need to take time off from work, or you could become completely unable to do certain tasks without putting your well-being at risk. Overworking yourself to the point of exhaustion could result in your work quality and productivity suffering. Your health is just as important as your mindset.

Taking a long-term view of your goals and your mindset also means taking a long-term view of your health. The small things you do every day that improve or hurt your health, add up over time. Grabbing a donut for breakfast or working late into the night to finish up a stressful project aren't great things to do for your health, even if they are only small lapses in judgment. You might be tempted to brush these things off as barely a drop in the bucket of your overall health, and if they only happened once or twice they might not have a big effect. However, if you repeat these bad health habits too often, they can become a much bigger problem. Looking at your health in the long-term means recognizing that actions and choices, that seem harmless at the moment, can actually be more damaging than you might think. They represent a pattern of bad behavior that can sneak up on you if you're not careful.

Don't just worry about your physical health either. While good physical health is something you should always strive for, your mental, emotional, and social health all play a role in your overall well-being too. Maintaining good mental health supports a positive, goal-oriented mindset. If you get too worn-down or you start thinking overly critically about yourself, you can become completely unmotivated, giving up on your goals and holding yourself back from success.

Your emotional health has to do with how you manage difficult emotions. If a temporary setback occurs and you feel upset or frustrated, what do you do with those feelings? If you allow them to overwhelm you, you impede your progress towards your goals. If you can properly manage anger, sadness, and the fear of failure, you will find it easier to recover from setbacks. Your social health is important too. Socializing isn't just a good idea for networking; it's also integral to your health. If you don't spend enough time with friends and family, you can get very burned out in your work very quickly. Managing all four of these aspects of your health is important if you want to achieve your goals.

Why Your Health Matters

The healthier we are, the easier it is to focus on our work and be productive. If we let negative emotions pile up, we can start doubting our abilities and talk ourselves out of new opportunities. If we eat poorly and don't exercise, we could put our physical health in jeopardy, which might lead to serious medical conditions. If we neglect our mental health and spend too much time working alone, not only do our productivity levels suffer (as well as our moods), but our families, communities, and businesses suffer as well when we don't take care of the only human vehicle we have: our bodies. Therefore, staying mentally, emotionally, socially, and physically healthy enables us to overcome these barriers and stay on track towards success.

Maintaining good long-term health ties into your happiness formula, which is "the unique mix of environmental factors and activities that are most likely to invigorate you and reset your energy batteries when they are running low" (Blake, 2017, para. 7). Maximizing your happiness formula involves fulfilling both your micro, daily needs and your macro, long-term needs. For example, something like taking a walk might be a micro need for your physical and mental health, while getting regular exercise would be a macro need. Spending some time with friends over the weekend is a micro need, while having a good relationship with your friends and family is a macro need. Just as small bad habits can add up to a larger negative effect, so too can small good habits add up to achieving maximum happiness and fulfillment in your life. If your happiness formula is high, you will be more productive and focused at work and at home.

How Your Health Applies to Your Goals

Good physical, mental, emotional, and social health allows us to get more done and get closer to achieving our goals. If you're in a terrible mood, your thoughts are cluttered, and you're feeling unmotivated, it can feel impossible to get started on a task. This is especially true if that task isn't something particularly fun. Your thoughts might keep leaping to all the other things you could be doing, making the current task take longer. You might become frustrated more easily, letting minor annoyances become major roadblocks that halt your progress. A task that should only take a matter of minutes ends up taking hours, or it gets ignored and forgotten until you can no longer put it off, forcing you to rush through it. Improving your health through the use of the happiness formula can help you refocus your mind, let go of agitation, and get some work done.

Think of your happiness and health needs like a mathematical equation. The happiness formula suggests that reaching maximum productivity is a matter of maximizing your happiness and ridding yourself of the things that are holding you back. This equation is "[(Ritual 1 + Ritual 2 + Ritual 3) x Booster] – Barrier/s to Drop = Daily Happiness" (Blake, 2017, para. 13). In order to better understand how you can achieve your daily happiness, let's first break down this formula.

Your rituals are the things you need to do each day to support your health and happiness. These might be some light exercise, eating a home-cooked meal, practicing a hobby, or anything else that helps you feel energized and balances your emotions. The booster or multiplier is a daily habit that "supercharges" your energy levels. Finally, identify a barrier in your life that brings you stress or gets in the way of your work. These barriers might be anxieties you feel over future work, failure, money troubles, or other sources of worry. They might also be bad habits you engage in like eating junk food, procrastinating, or spending time around toxic people.

Now that you know what each term in the equation means, you can fill it out for a reliable pathway to achieving daily happiness. Choose three daily rituals to complete, add in a booster activity, and work to get rid of a source of stress, and you will find yourself living a happier life that supports a healthier lifestyle. Your happiness formula doesn't have to be set in stone; you can change up the daily rituals if you are looking for some more variety, or you find that the old ones aren't working for you. The most effective daily formulas will keep you happy and focused, letting you knock out your short-term goals and make progress towards your long-term goals every day.

Overall Mindset Approach

Our health plays a key role in our mindset. If we are distracted by negative thoughts and bad habits, we lay a shaky foundation for the rest of our attitude. Poor health takes its toll on our overall well-being. It becomes harder to achieve our goals when we haven't fulfilled our health needs, whether those needs are physical or emotional.

Making a commitment to taking care of our health in the short-term sets us up for long-term success. Daily healthy choices create a pattern of good habits. Every good choice we make improves our overall happiness and makes us more motivated and productive. As we keep repeating good habits, and we improve and maintain our health, we no longer have to worry about poor health, nor are we distracted by self-critical thoughts or overwhelming emotions. It becomes easier to focus on our goals and ultimately achieve them.

Lifestyle Habits for Success: Routine, Discipline, and Focus

Establishing and practicing good habits is integral to our ability to succeed. Just like daily healthy habits lead to more long-term success, so too do daily productivity and lifestyle habits. These habits should focus on three key qualities: routine, discipline, and focus. Through these qualities, we can improve our work ethic and bring ourselves closer to success.

Establishing Routines

Establishing a good, consistent daily routine is great for your productivity. You can start each day with a good idea of what you need to get done and when you need to complete it. Routines naturally reinforce good behaviors because you repeat them every day, turning them into long-lasting habits. Rather than being a chore that you might be tempted to procrastinate, it's second nature to sit down and get some work done around the same time each day. The same is true for other daily tasks like eating, sleeping, and exercising, as well as relaxation time. If you go to bed and wake up at different times every day, your body isn't always ready for sleep at night, which can lead to staring up at the ceiling when you should be asleep. You can become tired and cranky from this lack of sleep, not to mention how your work quality can suffer too. If you stick to a good sleeping routine instead, it becomes easier to fall asleep and wake up around the same time each day. You will be better rested, leaving you ready to tackle whatever the day has to offer. Try to stick to a similar schedule each day, and you will find that making good lifestyle choices becomes nearly automatic.

You might think to yourself, isn't part of the benefit of being your own boss the ability to work whenever you want? While it is true that you can set your own hours, you should still do your best to make sure the hours you set for yourself are consistent. If you give yourself all day to get a task done without setting aside certain hours as "working hours" and others as "leisure time," work and play bleed into each other. It's harder to focus on work when you keep thinking about more fun things you could be doing, and even harder if you constantly interrupt your train of thought by switching back and forth between your work and another activity. You can choose the hours that are most comfortable for when you like to work, but make sure that they remain as consistent as possible so you can get more work done during these hours.

Routines and other lifestyle habits also help us hold ourselves accountable for starting and finishing our work. Actor Denzel Washington once said, "Without commitment you will never start, but more importantly, without consistency you will never finish" (Washington, 2017). Routines, discipline, and focus are most effective when they are used consistently. Without consistency, you can't turn these behaviors into powerful lifestyle habits. Apply these habits every day and you will be able to finish any task, no matter how large. If we always get started at a certain time, we resist the urge to put something off for even an hour or two. This gives us more time to complete the task before we reach the end of the time we have set aside to work. Scheduling your day also keeps you from overworking yourself. It is easy to get lost in work and end up toiling away long into the night. Sticking to your self-scheduled "working hours" ensures that you still find time for leisure, even on your busiest days. It keeps burnout at bay while still giving you enough time to get all of your work done comfortably.

For the best routines, schedule your entire day, including your mornings, afternoons, and evenings. Set aside certain tasks for specific parts of the day. For example, your morning routine should help you wake up, get energized, and get focused. A good morning routine might involve a refreshing shower, a filling breakfast, some light exercise to get your blood moving, and then getting right to work. Your afternoon routine should be all about maintaining your momentum and resisting the afternoon slump. Get the most important tasks done first, so they are always completed by the end of the day, and make sure to eat a healthy lunch, taking breaks to stand and stretch as needed. In the evening, start wrapping up your work and transitioning over to leisure time. Resist the urge to work long into the night; you could throw off your sleep schedule and fail to get enough rest to be at the height of productivity the next morning. Stick to your schedule at all hours so you can maximize your productivity and keep working towards your goals.

Developing Discipline

Maintaining a good routine requires you to have a lot of discipline. Discipline can be a tricky thing to cultivate, especially when there are so many temptations to avoid. Our lives are full of potential distractions and unhealthy behaviors. These include anything from grabbing an unhealthy snack, to making impulse purchases that reduce your savings, to avoiding work because it seems too difficult. Without discipline, we allow our impulsive thoughts and our desires for instant gratification to get in the way of our long-term goals. We are tempted to pursue momentary pleasure at the expense of achieving success later on. We might shirk our work to do something more fun like hang out with friends or watch a movie, even though we know we are only hurting ourselves in the long run.

When these temptations arise, we need to have the discipline to say no and make the right decision. We have to resist caving to distractions, and we must remain focused on our goals. If we can manage to stay the course, we make the best use of our time. We also show ourselves just how far hard work can get us. Even if procrastinating our work might have been more fun, it wouldn't have brought us any closer to achieving our goals. Additionally, procrastinating often results in doing more work in the long run as you never really achieve a level of success that would bring you financial security. If you can stay disciplined and avoid temptations in all forms, it will be easier to keep what really matters in mind.

Sometimes improving self-discipline is just a matter of finding the right motivation. Temptations are so powerful because they promise us instant gratification. They offer a brief moment of happiness which seems enjoyable at the time but which doesn't hold a candle to the long-term happiness you can achieve by working towards your life's purpose. When you think about hitting the snooze alarm or putting off work for another hour, think of what your work is helping you achieve in the long term. Think of how it is contributing to your big life goals, and how if you don't get your work done, you won't be able to achieve what you really want in life. Remind yourself of the reason why you need to keep working towards your goals—whether that reason is for your family's sake, for your own sense of fulfillment, to find financial freedom, or any combination of these motivators—and you'll find that temptations that once seemed so strong don't have much power over you after all.

Sharpening Your Focus

Distraction is the enemy of hard work. If your mind is constantly else-where, or worse, if you get up and leave in the middle of work to satisfy an impulse, you interrupt your work and throw yourself off your sched-ule. Improving your focus can help you avoid caving to distractions. It can also help you get "in the zone" when you are working, which typically produces a higher quality result. The longer you maintain your focus on one task, the faster you will typically complete that task.

Our lives are full of distractions. There is always a new TV show or movie to watch that can steal a few hours from our workday. Other people might call our attention away from our work. We even carry distractions around with us in the form of our phones. While these devices might be necessary in the modern world, they also make it very easy to lose minutes or hours to endless scrolling on social media and other apps. If we want to maintain our focus in the face of these and other distractions, we need to find a way to block them out or remove them from our surroundings.

This might mean putting up a "do not disturb" sign when we are working on something important and letting others know that we are in the middle of something, and we can get back to them later.

It might mean putting your phone on silent or turning it off so you aren't able to keep checking it. It could also mean removing sources of distraction like TVs and games from our workspace, so they can't catch our eye and tempt us. Cutting out these distractions allows us to keep our focus on our current task where it is needed most, helping us finish the task faster.

Multitasking is another form of distraction. Though it is often seen as a way to increase productivity, more often than not it actually makes you less productive because it interferes with your ability to give one task all of your attention. If you are constantly splitting your attention between two or more things, you never really get to focus on either one of them. You can reduce your working speed to a crawl and ruin the quality of your work as your mind struggles to repeatedly switch gears between the different tasks.

If you want to achieve maximum levels of productivity, focus on just one thing at a time. See that task through to its successful conclusion before taking on any other work. Even if you have multiple things you need to do in one day, take them one task at a time in order of greatest priority. It is only by keeping your focus narrowed to a single activity that you can get your work done with the greatest efficiency.

How to Apply Your Lifestyle Habits

Routines, discipline, and focus all play a role in keeping you on track to meet your goals. Without them, you will likely have trouble working efficiently and your productivity will suffer. When you learn to apply these positive lifestyle habits, you will notice a total change in the way you approach work. Instead of feeling like something you have to force yourself to do, work becomes something you might even feel excited to do.

These three key lifestyle habits all feed into each other. When combined, they greatly increase your ability to achieve success. Start out by writing down your daily routines. Plan out your day and make yourself a to-do list of the most important work that needs to get done. Next, apply discipline and focus to ensure you get your work done.

Resist the urge to procrastinate work in favor of more "fun" activities. Reinforce your motivation to stick to your routine, and get your work done by thinking about how each task on your to-do list brings you closer to achieving your short-term and long-term goals.

The better you get at blocking out distractions, the more focused you will be as you work. Additionally, having a clear routine makes it easier to exercise restraint and avoid distractions. Tackling your work by utilizing a list reduces the chances of trying to multitask. It improves your focus by encouraging you to work on one thing at a time. When you apply each of these lifestyle habits, you provide yourself with a recipe for success.

Overall Mindset Approach

Big changes are the product of many smaller decisions. Adopting good lifestyle habits can turn a complex, difficult task into something more easily accomplished. Habits are an amazing way to get a little bit closer to your goals every day. You can use them to complete any large task that would otherwise feel overwhelming. If you get into the habit of making just a little progress towards a larger goal each day, you will eventually arrive at the finish line. Through using routines, developing discipline, and sharpening your focus, you can tackle many short-term goals on your way to greater success.

While it's important to always keep our long-term goals in mind, our short-term goals represent the steps on the path to these long-term goals. Like the positive habits we adopt in our daily lives, they help us make a little bit of progress towards becoming a successful CDL entrepreneur with enough money and control over our lives to accomplish even greater goals. These good habits show us how there is no goal too great for us to accomplish as long as we start small, think big, and build our way up to making a large-scale change in our lives.

The Power of Executing Smart Goals

Having goals is great, but taking the time to clearly define them and understand how you will go about achieving them is even better. Say your dream is to run your own business. If you never really develop your goal more than this, you aren't very likely to achieve it. Without setting up a clear timeline for achieving this goal, you might keep pushing it back, possibly never achieving it at all. Without fully understanding what the conditions for success are and what you would have to do to run your own company, you might assume much more work is required, or you might think the opposite and assume the task will be much easier than it actually is. Just like any assignment, you need to understand what is expected of you and how long you have to complete the task, even if the due date is only enforced by yourself. In order to set achievable goals, you must consider what you need to accomplish to get closer to your goal, develop a clear plan, and give yourself a deadline.

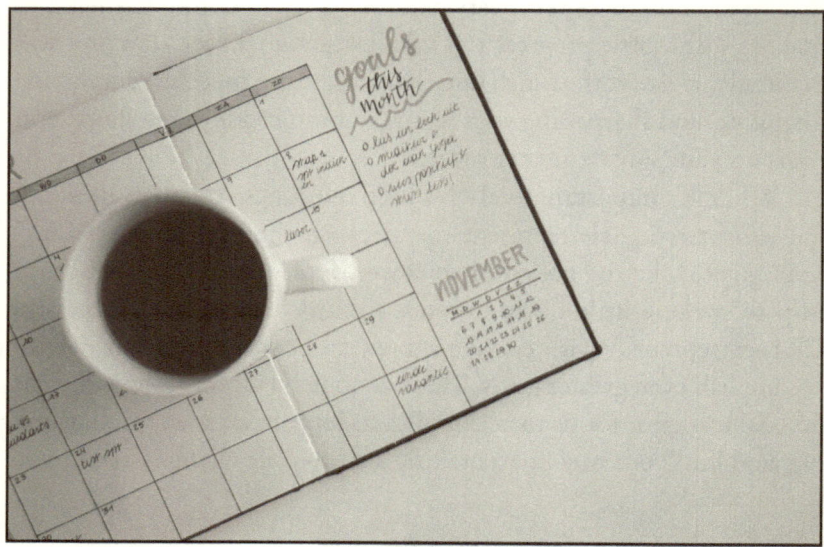

Proper planning goes a long way toward setting and achieving goals more efficiently. When you actually make an action plan for your long-term goals, you are much more likely to achieve them. In order to do this, you must learn to set and execute smart goals.

Setting smart goals helps you work smarter, not harder. According to Zig Ziglar, a successful salesman, author, and motivational speaker, the process of setting goals and successfully achieving them can be broken down into seven steps. His goal setting canvas outlines each of these steps and how they can help you create a plan of attack for even the most difficult goals. His steps include identifying the goal, listing the benefits of achieving the goal, listing the obstacles in your way, identifying the skills and knowledge you will need, looking for people who will help you achieve your goals, creating a step-by-step plan, and setting a deadline.

Identify the Goal

The first step in setting goals is deciding what you want to achieve. You need to set a target so you can aim towards that target in everything that you do. This step typically requires some self-reflection so you can identify your life's purpose and the goals that will help you be the person you want to be.

When identifying what you want in life, make sure you choose specific goals. As Ziglar says, "If you want to have specific success you must have specific targets" (Ziglar, n.d., para. 1). If you aim too broad, it will be difficult to know when you've achieved your goals. For example, saying that you want to become more productive is a good thing to aim for, but it's not a specific enough goal. What would being more productive look like for you? A better goal might be to commit yourself to getting your work done at the beginning of the day, or to double the amount of work you currently do. Similarly, wanting to have more money is another non-specific goal. Is having an extra dollar enough to qualify as "more money"? How can you tell? Pick something more specific, like setting a goal to have three months' worth of your current salary in your savings account. Specific goals give you something concrete to aim for and you get a clear idea of exactly when you have achieved your goal.

List the Benefits—What's in it for me?

Why does your goal matter to you? What really drives you to accomplish it? If you don't think that achieving your goal will help you, you won't have much motivation to keep working towards it. Listing out all of the benefits you will get from achieving a goal shows you why the goal is worth fighting for. These benefits might include financial freedom, more security for your family, or a sense of satisfaction and fulfillment.

It might initially feel a bit self-centered to wonder what's in it for you, but the truth is that your goals need to have personal significance. If you are trying to achieve them because it's what someone else expects you to do, you're not going to have the motivation you need to keep pushing for them when things get tough. Think of all the people who go to medical school or law school because their parents expect them to be doctors or lawyers, but who end up dropping out because they had no passion for the work they were doing. If you choose goals that you genuinely care about achieving and that bring you some personal benefit, you can push through even the toughest of obstacles in your path to success.

List the Obstacles to Overcome

No matter what you're trying to achieve, you're probably going to face some obstacles. While you can't predict everything, making a list of the most likely issues you will face will help you mentally prepare yourself for the challenge and devise a plan for overcoming them. It might seem like immediately listing out all the hardships you might encounter is a good way to demotivate yourself, but it's actually better to start working on your goals knowing that challenges are an unavoidable part of the process. If you let common problems blindside you and you fail to prepare for them, it is much harder to deal with them. If you know what could be coming, you can decide what you're going to do about it long before it ever becomes a problem.

If you're trying to break into the CDL field and start your own business, you will need to overcome some obstacles. For starters, you're going to need enough money to get the company off the ground. You could have some initial difficulties securing customers. You might have trouble finding enough employees to meet your customers' demands, or finding the right employees that fit in well with your company vision. It can take some time to reach a point where you are comfortable managing your company, and it's okay if you don't achieve immediate success. These issues are much easier to accept and deal with when you know about them in advance.

List the Skills and Knowledge Required

Now that you have a good idea of some of the obstacles keeping you from reaching your goal, think about the skills you would need to overcome these obstacles. Each goal requires a different skill set, as well as learning new information in a different area. The skills you need to cultivate if you want to learn to cook are very different from those you need to learn to run your own CDL business. Identify the skills and information that are the most important to your goal and take every opportunity to expand your abilities in these areas.

Identify the People and Groups to Work With

We can go very far on our own with enough self-discipline and skill, but not nearly as far as we can go with the help of others. Other people can lend us their skills and knowledge, allowing us to get more done and helping us in areas where we're not experts. Collaborators, mentors and advisors, team members, and employees can all assist us on our journey to success. Consider where your weaknesses lie and how other people can help you overcome these weaknesses.

When you run a business, you need to learn how to delegate. You aren't going to be able to do everything by yourself. Delegating involves finding the right person for every job, even and especially if that person isn't you. If you're not especially great at accounting, hire someone to deal with the company's finances. If you find you're spending far too much time on routine customer service, hire someone who can answer customer questions and provide them with the resources they're looking for. Even getting someone to answer the phone for you reduces the amount of time you waste each day, leaving you with more time to focus on the work that only you can do. Starting a company is a team effort. Fill your team with like-minded people and groups who will help you achieve your goals.

Develop a Plan of Action

You know what you need to do and you know the challenges you will face in your journey. It's time to develop your action plan for achieving your goals.

A good plan can save you a lot of trouble. In fact, making a plan is the most important step in the process of making smart goals. Without one, you have a goal in mind but no idea how you're going to get there. Think of it like getting in the car with a destination in mind but no instructions for how to get there. You could waste plenty of time driving around in circles and taking the wrong exits. Your plan is like the GPS that guides you towards your destination, always keeping you on the right track. Once you have your GPS, you can simply follow its instructions; you don't have to worry if every turn you make is the right one because you've already planned out your journey.

To write out your plan, think about the details of how you will achieve your goal. Look at the big steps you'll have to take, then break them down into the small steps that contribute to the bigger ones. For example, if one of your big steps is getting enough money to start your company, the smaller tasks might include researching how much money you will need, running a fundraiser, looking for investors, and taking out personal loans to cover the rest. Breaking a big task down into these bite-sized tasks makes it less intimidating and more manageable. Once you've done this for each step in your plan, you will end up with something that is clear and easy to follow. With a detailed plan, it is only a matter of time until you reach your goal.

Set a Deadline for Achievement

When you understand what you want to achieve and how much work will go into achieving it, you can figure out how long it might take you to reach your goals. Setting a deadline makes you accountable for getting your work done. Without it, you will procrastinate on getting started. A deadline creates a sense of urgency, encouraging you to get started right away and not waste any more time.

While your deadline should matter, it's okay if things take a bit longer and you end up making adjustments to it later on. It gives you a good goal to shoot for, but unexpected circumstances can get in the way of your initial estimates. If you need to, readjust your time frame as you get a better understanding of how realistic your initial predictions were.

Using the Goal Sheet

Ziglar's goal sheet is an indispensable tool for making progress on your goals. You can use it to organize every step of the goal-planning process. The goal sheet allows you to be more prepared for the challenges you will face, reinforcing your determination, and making you a more effective entrepreneur.

Once you've filled out the goal sheet, pin it somewhere in your office, or wherever you work, so that you can easily refer back to it. If you're ever at a loss for what to do next, look back at your goal sheet and identify your next step. If you're ever feeling unmotivated, remember all of the reasons you are trying to achieve your goals. If you ever find you need a little help, refer back to the list of people and groups who could help you. Keeping the sheet on hand lets you look back at it whenever you need some guidance or motivation so you can get right back to work.

Overall Mindset Approach

The motivational benefit of getting our goals down on paper cannot be understated. It seems like a small step, but writing down our goals really does make us more committed to seeing them through. Our goals go from pleasant daydreams to something we see as achievable, all because we took the time to plan out how we would achieve them. Setting smart goals trains our brains to think of these goals as not just something we want but something we will achieve. Adding a deadline allows us to anticipate the resolution of all of our efforts, which makes it all the easier to get moving on the goals we might have been putting off for months or years.

When we write out a plan, we become much more likely to follow it. We learn exactly how much work our goals will take, and we often find that it is less work than we initially anticipated. When we see that the barrier for success is much lower than we initially assumed, we can get right to work on achieving our life's purposes without hesitation.

Overall Mindset Going Forward

"Life is 10% what happens to you and 90% how you react to it"—Charles R. Swindoll

Your mindset is the foundation of your success. It is what encourages you to start working towards your goals, and it is what will keep you moving no matter what comes next. In your journey to start your own CDL company and accomplish every other long-term goal you set, you are going to face hardships. There are going to be times when you might want to give up. In these moments, the right mindset is the difference between throwing in the towel and finding a way to overcome the challenge. When you believe in your ability to achieve success, and you see everything you can accomplish by moving forward, you will never want to take a step back again.

Becoming CDL-Minded means making the choice to take a proactive role in your own life. It means making the best of any situation and always working towards improving your life, whether it's through establishing and managing your company, or living a fulfilling personal life. Difficulties are inevitable, but how you choose to respond to these difficulties makes all the difference. You can allow the speed bumps and obstacles you encounter to throw you off course. You can adopt a "woe is me" attitude and give up on trying to make your life any better. Or, you can react to whatever life throws at you by maintaining a positive outlook. You can counter misfortune with a can-do attitude and plenty of perseverance. As long as you have a good attitude and a good mindset, there is no difficulty too great for you to overcome.

STEP 2

CDL-Minded in YOUR 'Business'

The 'GAME' Plan for Your Business

The smart goals discussed in the previous chapter work so well because you can use them to create a path for you to follow. Achieving your goals doesn't have to be a guessing game. The way ahead is clear and you know exactly how to proceed because you have created an actionable plan for yourself.

This same method of breaking things down into actionable steps can be used for your business as well. Starting and running a business is a major venture, and it's hard to know exactly where to start and how you're going to expand once you've launched your business. It's critical that you take the time to plan out the steps you will take in a way that is easy to follow and that fits neatly with your vision for your company. To do this, you don't just need a business plan. You need a GAME plan.

What is the GAME Plan?

The GAME plan is an acronym that represents the key components of any good actionable plan for your company. It emphasizes setting specific goals rather than overly general ones that are easy to ignore, as well as making sure your goals are reasonable and measurable. It also encourages you to create a plan that makes you excited to get started right away.

The GAME plan is a deceptively simple formula that produces shockingly powerful results. It is made up of four components. These are making your plan goal-centric, choosing actionable steps, picking goals that are measurable, and setting effective goals and steps toward those goals that you can execute right away.

Goal

We've talked a lot about goal setting so far, but what really is a goal? What makes for a great goal and what makes for a weak one? When you set your goals for your company, what kind of goals should you set?

A great goal is an expectation that you set for yourself. It is something you hold yourself accountable for completing, and something that you believe you will eventually achieve. It is an idea that you envision as part of your future, and ideally it is something that you care deeply about achieving or something that will help you reach other goals you care about. Goals are planned out and acted upon to turn your desires into reality.

When setting company goals, consider all of these factors. Is the goal you set something you actually see yourself achieving, or does it sound impossible? While you can always shoot for the stars, you should try to choose goals that you believe you can accomplish, even if this requires a great deal of hard work. For example, setting a goal of making your company the most successful business in the CDL industry seems motivating at first because you will always work to be the best. However, in practice it can actually be hard to motivate yourself to do this because it is so difficult that your brain tunes it out. You stop holding yourself accountable for it because it feels impossible. A better goal might be to establish a company that generates a profit within the first year, or that makes a certain amount. This goal, while still requiring some work, is definitely achievable, which is a greater incentive for you to complete it.

Actionable

It's all too easy to get advice that isn't specific enough to help. Say your goal was to get in shape and the article you read simply said to start exercising. Exercise should definitely be a part of your plan, but how should you implement it? How long should you exercise for, and what kinds of exercise are best for your specific fitness goals? Without clear, actionable advice, you could make missteps or fail to get started at all because you don't know what's expected of you. If you don't make the plan for achieving your company goals actionable, you could run into the same problem in your business.

An actionable goal is something you can take steps to achieve right now. It is a plan you can realistically put into action as you move forward. It is also one that you have clearly planned out to the extent that you could hand your plan to anyone else, and they could follow it. You want to give yourself specific steps so you don't waste any time wondering what you should do next, and the steps you choose should lead to your goal.

See where you can turn parts of your plan into more actionable steps. If you want to improve the employee training process so new hires know exactly what is expected of them, some actionable steps might be creating a training process that is the same for each employee in a certain job, creating a new employee manual, and writing up step-by-step guides for their first few days on the job. If you want to find more customers, some actionable steps might include creating an online advertising campaign, renting billboard space, or sending out fliers. These goals give you something specific you can do right now to get closer to your long-term goals

Measurable

Another common pitfall when setting goals is failing to make your goals measurable. Setting a measurable goal means you will know exactly when you have achieved it. It is the difference between saying you want to lose some weight and saying you want to lose 10 pounds. You get a clear finish line and you can track your progress toward it every step of the way. Additionally, measurable goals should have a clear deadline. Do you want to lose those 10 pounds in two months or five years? Giving yourself a deadline helps you see if you are making good progress toward achieving your goal on time, or if you need to pick up the pace. Measurable goals are also easier to update once you've achieved them, as you can just increase the numbers and give yourself a new target to shoot for.

Measurable goals are just as important for your business as they are everywhere else. If you decide you want your company to make $10,000 in profit in the first year, you can easily check on your progress every few months and make sure you're still on track to achieve your goal. When you succeed, you can update your goal to $20,000 in profits next year, and keep scaling your goals to match the amount that you want your company to grow.

Effective

Finally, the goals you set should be effective at getting you motivated and encouraging you to take action. You should be able to take the plan you have made and get working on it right away. Even if you cannot do everything on your list on day one, you should at least be able to start with a few tasks and work your way up towards everything else as your company finds its footing.

As you begin to execute your plan, you may find that some steps are more difficult than you initially assumed. It's okay if you have to go back and rework some of your time frames, or you need to break a single step down into smaller ones, in order to accomplish it. If the setback interferes with your motivation, refer back to all of the benefits you will receive as you achieve your goals, and how your company will continue to expand. When you finally reach success, all of the work will have been worth it.

Writing a Company Game Plan

A great company game plan is much more than just a set of steps to follow. It gives your business a real purpose, bringing it closer to your personal mission and vision statement. There is a big difference between a business plan and a real game plan. While a business plan might be used to secure finances or tell others what your company does, your game plan should be primarily written for your own use. It is a way to lay out your goals and projections for the future, making them easier to achieve and also ensuring they line up with your personal goals. Your game plan is to, for, and within your business. It will help guide your decisions and show others what your company is really about, not just how much money it makes.

Of course, money can be part of your game plan too, since it's a part of many goals. One of the greatest benefits of owning a company in the CDL industry is the financial freedom you will enjoy once your company is up and running. Recent estimates say that as a company owner, "you can average about $184,803 per year," not to mention the benefits you'll receive from a recent tax reform plan that pledges "the corporate tax rate will be lowered, a repatriation plan will be in place," and a change to "the way that pass-through business income is taxed" (TanTara, 2019, para. 5-10) in your favor. This all adds up to a very nice paycheck that can help you achieve your other goals as long as you establish and stick to a solid company game plan. Your plan should start with a company ethos that parallels your life's purpose.

Writing a Mission and Vision Statement That Aligns with Your Life's Purpose

If you want to achieve your life's purpose, you need to make the first move. Your company's mission statement should set you up to follow through on your purpose. While there is plenty to look forward to in your future, "it can only be brought into manifestation through desire, faith, or the spoken word" (Shinn, 2005, p. 12). What this means for your company is that while you can achieve great things, opportunities may slip out of your hands if you do not take the proper steps to take advantage of them. You need to put your will out into the universe to get your wishes fulfilled.

Your vision statement is a great way to express your desires to yourself and those around you. It should outline what you want to achieve and why it is so important to get there. Your reasons why should all come from your life's purpose. How does achieving each goal you set for your company bring you closer to your personal and professional goals? How does it help you make an impact on your own life, the lives of your family members, and the lives of those in your community? For example, having a profitable company and plenty of extra money could help you put your kids through college. It could also help you give back to your community or donate money to charitable causes you support. A great mission statement matters to you, as well as your customers, because it shows how your company's success can benefit everyone.

The Importance of Your Business' Mission Statement

We have already discussed how a mission statement can help guide the decisions you make as the leader of your company, and this is still very true. You should try to make decisions that follow through on what you promised in your mission statement, as doing so helps you get closer to achieving your goals. A truly great mission statement, that you hold close to your heart as you make important decisions, also has the hidden advantage of helping out with marketing.

People want to care about your business for reasons other than price or even quality of service. This is the reason why businesses closely tied to charitable causes can often charge a bit more for their services. Customers know that a portion of the profits help to make a positive difference in the world. If customers feel like supporting your business improves their community, or that the money they spend is going to a good cause, they are more likely to choose your company over other options. Hearing a sweet story about how your company is helping kids lead better lives, and the money you make is being used to improve other families' lives, is heartwarming. Wouldn't you want to support a business like that? Having a clear vision and life's purpose for your company encourages brand loyalty and positive word-of-mouth marketing, and great marketing is key to any successful business.

Of all the things you can do for your business, marketing is the most important one. It is absolutely vital for success. Without it, you limit the number of potential customers who see your company and consider choosing it for their needs. If no one knows your company exists, or if you don't have a way to stand out from the crowd of other similar companies, you're going to have a hard time establishing yourself in the CDL market. If you market yourself in a way that helps you really connect with your customers by emphasizing the greater purpose of your company, you will build a loyal base of patrons and attract droves of new customers.

How to Apply Your Mission Statement to Your Business

Once you've come up with a mission statement and purpose for your business, you just need to follow through with it. When you face a difficult decision and you don't know what choice to make, choose the one that aligns closest to your company's vision. When you are trying to expand your company, expand in a way that brings you closer to your company's long-term goals. If you are consistent in your choices, your company will get closer to your vision every day. You will not only create a game plan but also follow through on it.

Registering Your Company as a Cooperative Business or LLC

Now that you've laid the groundwork for your company, it's time to actually establish it. As a small business, you'll want to register your company as a cooperative business (co-op) or a limited liability company (LLC). Doing so offers you greater protections for your personal property, as well as legal and tax advantages. LLCs are a good choice for small businesses. Compared to corporations, they are typically easier to set up, less expensive, and they offer more flexibility.

Registering your business is easier than it sounds. First, you need to appoint a registered agent. The registered agent is the "official point of contact" for the business, and they're required to "sign for and receive legal notices, state mandates, wage garnishments, and tax documents during specific business hours" (Incorporate.com, n.d., para. 7) for the state. You can take this job on yourself or give the responsibility to someone else, but whoever you choose, make sure they will be available when the state calls on them to complete these tasks. If you think you'll be too busy running things, you can appoint a trustworthy business partner instead.

To register as an LLC, you'll also need an employer identification number (EIN). This is used to identify your business and it allows you to open a bank account for your company. You'll also need your EIN for filing taxes. Obtaining an EIN is part of the process of filing your company with the state.

Some, but not all, states require you to create an LLC operating agreement. This is a blueprint for the internal structure of your company. It details who has ownership of the company, the rights of different members, and how profits and losses are distributed, for example. Check with your state and local laws to see if this is a necessary part of your registration process.

Prior to completing these tasks, however, you'll need to decide what kind of LLC you want to register your company as.

Choosing the Right Type of LLC

The type of LLC that's right for your business is largely dependent on the size and structure of your business. There are a few different kinds of LLCs, but you only need to choose between the three most relevant ones for CDL businesses. These are single-member LLCs, general partnerships, and family limited partnerships. The option you choose is based on who you want to have a say, legally, in how your company operates.

As the name implies, single-member LLCs, also known as sole proprietorship businesses, are owned and operated by a single person. You alone would be responsible for any sales your company makes, as well as any taxes and debts the business owes. If you are starting your business with another person or multiple business partners, the general partnership is a better fit for your needs. Each co-owner shares the responsibility for the company's assets and expenses. If you want your business to be a family venture, register as a family limited partnership. With this structure, you can easily transfer control to different members of the family, making it easier to pass down the family business.

Making Your LLC Work for You

The most important benefit that comes with forming an LLC is that it provides protection for you and your assets. When you register your company as an LLC, you separate the company's finances from your own. You still pay yourself from your company's profits, but the resources available to your company and your resources as an individual are treated as two separate entities under the law.

This may not seem like an important distinction, but it can actually make a huge difference in terms of liability. Let's say your business generates debt, or a lawsuit is filed against the company. The liability for paying any associated fees now falls on the company, not you.

Debts can only be demanded from your company's bank account and other assets, not your own. This means unless you choose to pay these debts out of your personal bank account, you can't be ordered to pay more than what's in your company's account. You will also avoid having valuable resources like your home or personal car repossessed for a debt incurred by your business. This protection is incredibly valuable for you as a business owner, so forming an LLC is worth the cost and minor hassle of filing the paperwork.

Forming an LLC protects you from a few other liabilities as well. These include liability for your co-owners' actions and your employees' actions if they commit fraud, injure someone, or otherwise act recklessly while they are affiliated with the business. Additionally, if you have personal debts, none of your company's resources can be repossessed to pay these debts without your consent.

Overall Mindset Approach

As the owner of your own company, your actions impact more people than just yourself. You also invite some risk into your life when you start a business. There is every chance that you will find success and wealth with your new company, but there is always a chance, no matter how small, that your company could fail. If you don't take the proper steps to protect yourself from the fallout of significant debt, lawsuits, or bankruptcy, you, your company, and your employees are all at major risk. By forming an LLC, this will allow you to take the necessary steps to protect your assets and look out for your company, and it's a major step you absolutely don't want to skip.

CHAPTER
3

The Secrets to Small Businesses Vs. Large Businesses

The CDL industry is full of businesses, both small and large in scale. Some CDL companies employ fleets of truckers and provide service across the entire nation, while others service a smaller area, such as providing school buses for the schools in a county, or shuttling people to and from work in a certain city. There is a common belief that the bigger your company is, the better, but is this really true? Is it impossible to succeed as a small business, or are there actually some advantages to starting small?

As a small business, it can often feel difficult to compete with larger businesses that may have a greater share of the market than you do. You might feel like you are a small fish in a huge pond full of much bigger fish. You may think that there's no way you can compete with these bigger businesses. The truth is that even though they may have more resources at their disposal, you can still run an incredibly successful small business that is very profitable. In fact, in some ways it is actually better to be a small business because you don't have to deal with many of the difficulties that come with a larger-scale operation. This can give you more control over what you want your company to be and how you will direct its growth.

Learning how to make a small business as profitable as its larger counterparts is a matter of learning to leverage your time in the best way possible. Rather than focusing on trivial matters and small improvements, you need to learn where you can make the biggest improvements to your company by spending the least amount of time. In order to do this, you must also understand what differentiates small businesses from large ones, and how many people have found success running businesses with a more limited scope. If you leverage your time properly, and use the resources you have to your advantage, you can compete with even the largest CDL businesses.

Small and Large Businesses

Just like in any other field, knowing your competition will give you some insight as to how you can find your own place in the market. It's important to understand both the many different kinds of small businesses you might want to create, as well as the differences between these businesses and larger ones. It's also a good idea to get a sense of the similarities that small and large businesses in the CDL industry share. Through this process, you can get an idea of how you can use the unique differences that being a small business provides to your advantage, as well as how you can capitalize on the similarities. Getting a good sense of what the CDL field looks like as a whole, will help you better understand your place in it and assist you in carving out a niche for yourself.

Types of Small CDL Businesses

There are many different kinds of jobs that require a CDL, and there are equally as many types of businesses in the CDL industry. These jobs may involve the transportation of various goods or people across vastly different sized areas. While some jobs are more suited to larger enterprises, such as countrywide delivery along the lines of FedEx and

UPS, there are plenty of CDL businesses you can operate on a smaller scale when you are just starting out.

If you don't have much money for start-up costs, there are still some CDL businesses you can run with limited resources. A moving company could be a great place to start, as you just need a large vehicle with storage space, somewhere to park it, and someone to assist with lifting heavy objects. While larger companies like UHaul exist, you can differentiate yourself by providing higher-quality service to a smaller region. Other ideas that are relatively cheap to start include running a small-scale shuttle service for commuters if you live near a big city, or running a tour bus if you're based near a popular destination.

In addition to the previous two options, there are many types of CDL companies that are influenced by where you live. For example, if you live near a lake or ocean you might operate a boat towing service. If there is an airport nearby, you might make your money with a company that shuttles people to and from their planes, especially if the airport is underserved by taxis. You might even look into transporting livestock if you live somewhere more rural.

Many CDL companies work alongside other industries. Waste hauling, water hauling, and septic hauling are all examples of this symbiotic relationship. Furniture delivery is another option if you are interested in contracting with stores that aren't big enough to offer their own service. You might start a similar business that helps haul large appliances to and from peoples' homes. Hauling large, bulky construction equipment is another viable option, as well as starting a towing company, provided you get the right permits for each.

No matter where your interests lie or where you live, there are plenty of ways to start working in the CDL industry even if you don't yet have the money to buy a whole fleet of trucks or shuttles. Choose a type of business that is interesting to you, and that helps bring you closer to achieving your goals without sacrificing the things that matter most.

Differences Between Running Small and Large Businesses

There are many differences between small and large businesses, especially at the company ownership level. While large businesses may have the capability to generate more money, there are also plenty of problems unique to these large companies. Running a large business means keeping track of hundreds or even thousands of different clients, not to mention just as many employees. It means business owners either spreading themselves thin or delegating tasks to others who may or may not complete them to their approval. People who own large businesses may need to spend more time at work just to manage everything at their companies, which means less free time to spend with friends and family. While there may be more cash flow, there is less opportunity to enjoy the benefits of owning their own business.

When you have a small business, many of these growing pains disappear because there is a lot less for you to keep track of. You will likely only manage a handful of other employees, and if you need to delegate any work, you can choose someone you trust to take over the responsibility. You have more control over your business and how daily operations are run. You also have greater control over your life as a whole as there are fewer demands on your time. While you may still look to expand your small business, operating at a small scale isn't always a bad thing.

Small businesses also get to enjoy the benefits of being classified as an LLC, which is much less complex than registering a huge company. While you will still have to pay some LLC registration fees, these fees are much cheaper than what larger companies pay. You also don't have to worry about nearly the same risk of liability, which gives you a little more freedom for how you want your company to operate.

Similarities Between Running Small and Large Businesses

Though there are plenty of differences, small and large businesses in the CDL industry have some things in common as well. Running either type of business can provide you with a sizable income that opens many future paths for you. A CDL business of any size can help you break out of a routine job that leaves you exhausted for an average paycheck. You can achieve a startling level of success in the commercial driving industry, whether you run and maintain a small company, or you work your way up to a large fleet of drivers that service many different customers.

The main thing that small and large businesses have in common is the need for passion and a good mindset. At the end of the day, small or large, these are all companies in the same industry. Genuine appreciation for CDL jobs ties the industry together, and the best leaders in businesses of all sizes have adopted the CDL-Minded approach. If you have a goal-oriented state of mind and you really care about your business, you will fit right in no matter the size of your company.

How to Utilize These Resources to Your Advantage

As a small business, you're not going to have access to the same number of resources that bigger companies get. You may not have very many employees, and as a result you may be limited in the number of customers you can take on at the beginning. Part of expanding your business is learning to work with the resources you have and maximize your profits, even in a small-scale company.

Owning a small business doesn't mean you can't succeed. It just means that you have to be smarter about using the resources at your disposal. You may not have access to a fleet of hundreds of trucks, but you can buy a few trucks, and ensure that the drivers for each truck are providing the highest quality of service. You may not have many people working under you that can manage whole sections of your company for you, but this just means that you get more direct control over every part of your business. As a small company, you can shape your company so it best fits the purpose you outlined in your mission statement.

CDL-Minded Approach

In commercial driving companies, success can be found in a wide variety of businesses. The typical image that CDL brings to mind, of driving a truck all across the country, is a viable option, but it's far from the only one. Because of this, anyone in the CDL industry can succeed, no matter how much money you have when you founded your company. You can start with a small operation of just a handful of people, and slowly grow it over time into a business that makes well over $100,000 a year. Both small and large businesses can find success, so long as you make proper use of your resources.

One of the most important resources to learn how to manage is time. If you want to achieve great success, learn to leverage your time to best suit your needs. Many people believe that it's better to spend time to save money, but it's actually better and effective to spend money to save yourself some time. While saving time can help you make your money back, saving money can't rewind the clock. When you use your time effectively you will see an amazing return on your investments, no matter how large your business is.

The Art of Leveraging Time

The common misconception of time is that "time is the most valuable resource." While time is certainly an important resource, it isn't nearly as valuable as energy. Your energy impacts everything you do, from how much work you can get done in a day to how much passion you have for your business. Without energy, you could have all the time in the world and still not get anything done. It can even help you manage your time well and use it efficiently, which allows you to properly leverage your time. How you use your energy and time will determine how valuable your resources are and how successful you can be.

When you leverage your time well, you apply your energy to the areas that need it most. This helps you focus on what matters, and you get the greatest effect for the least amount of time spent. You only have so much energy every day. Overworking yourself and ending up exhausted doesn't do your productivity any favors. It's better to use your time and energy wisely and work on the most important things first, while you still have the energy to get them done. In order to do this, you need to identify the areas with the greatest potential for growth in your business.

One of the biggest obstacles to leveraging your time effectively is focusing on the wrong things. If you let the small stuff get in the way, you could end up wasting all of your time and energy on something that is only going to provide a little bit of growth for your company. For example, say you put a lot of energy into improving your negotiation skills. You read books about charisma and making deals, you attend seminars, and you get plenty of practice negotiating. This might let you negotiate slightly better contracts, but how much does that help you in the long run? Is it better to make a few extra dollars from a handful of contracts, or would it be better to attract many new customers and double the number of contracts your company has? The latter option has a much higher growth potential and it will make you more money for less effort.

In proper time management, you want to look at the things that are going to have the biggest impact on your success. Keep the big picture in mind and always look for ways that you can get closer to your long-term goals; don't get bogged down by short-term solutions. Instead of putting all your energy into negotiation skills, it might be a better investment of your time and energy to focus on marketing so you can reach more customers. You can make more money than you ever could from making tiny improvements to the terms of each contract. From there, you'll build a more long-lasting business, if you expand your customer base. While negotiation is still a good skill to have under your belt, pursue it only if it will make the biggest impact on your business. Looking at the long-term effects of how you spend your time will help you make the right calls.

How to Effectively Leverage Your Time

Effective time management requires you to be able to set priorities for your tasks. You want to work on the important things first, and save everything else for later, or you risk wasting energy on things that are less important. If you have a lot of work to get done, consider what will bring you the greatest gain by finishing it, and what will have the greatest consequences if you don't get it done by the end of the day. Work on these tasks first, even and especially if they are the hardest tasks. You have the most energy right at the beginning of the day, so use it in the best possible way and make the best use of your time.

Delegation is another key component of good time management. For every task, consider who would be best suited for the job. This could be you, or it could be someone else in your company. Learning to identify "the skills, knowledge and abilities you possess and spending your time leveraging these talents will provide you with the most productive and profitable impact" (Gatty, 2017, para. 2). Know what you're good at and know what others are good at, and assign each task to the person who will do the best job. If you're not strong with finances, delegate the task to someone who is, or hire someone for the job. If you're great at employee oversight, focus on that, and leave routine paperwork and answering the phones to someone else. When done correctly, delegation keeps you from wasting time on tasks you aren't great at and lets you spend your energy where it is most needed.

While you want your company to operate efficiently, you should prioritize effectiveness. Efficiency means you are completing tasks as quickly as possible. While this is good, it doesn't always allow for you to determine if the tasks you're doing are actually worth doing. You don't want to just fill your schedule. You want to focus on the tasks that actually matter and cut out busy work wherever you can in order to make your business more effective. Consider whether lengthy processes need to be done at all or if there's a better alternative. Figure out if you can train others to do tasks and free up your own time to focus on big-picture activities. Look for alternatives to spending excessive time and energy on tasks. All of this ensures that your business is operating as effectively as possible.

The Overall Mindset Approach

The idea of running a small business can feel very limiting. You may initially feel that there's no way you can compete with bigger businesses, and you may have concerns about getting pushed out of the market. However, with energy management skills and a goal-oriented mindset, you can still run a highly successful and competitive company.

When you really consider the advantages and disadvantages of running a small business compared to a larger one, you will start to see that, if you manage your resources right, a small business can still help you achieve success. Learning to leverage your time effectively helps you make the best use of your resources, even if you have access to fewer resources than large companies. If you work to become the best company you can be at your current scale, you can expand your business over time or just maximize your effectiveness as a small business. Either way, you will have plenty of opportunities to keep working towards your life's purpose.

CHAPTER 4

Expenses You MUST KNOW in Your CDL Business

As much as running a CDL business can be a labor of love, at the end of the day it is also a company that needs to remain profitable in order to continue operating. If you want to run a successful business, you need to consider the financial aspect, and that means accounting for all of the expenses your company will generate. If you want to turn a profit, you need to know how much money you're going to spend just to get things running.

The type and scale of your business will have an impact on how much it costs to operate. Larger businesses generally cost more, though they can bring in more money as well. Smaller businesses are usually much cheaper to run, but the expenses they do have are still important to consider. Different kinds of CDL businesses will cost different amounts as well. It might be cheaper to run a small tour bus company that only requires two or three buses and a small staff, than it is to run a delivery company where more drivers and more trucks are needed. Still, as long as you account for the expenses in your industry, you can make enough money that these costs aren't a problem. If you make smart financial decisions that account for common sources of debt in the CDL industry, you can keep your business highly profitable.

Common Expenses in the CDL Industry

While the details of the expenses that each company has to worry about are a little different, there are some common expenses that are present in almost all CDL businesses, no matter the service they provide or their size. Knowing what these expenses are and how much they can cost, you can better prepare you to make a financial plan that helps you offset these costs. Consider how each of these expenses might affect your own business.

Vehicles

All CDL businesses have vehicle expenses. Whether your business uses trucks, vans, buses, shuttles, or any other type of commercial vehicle, buying the vehicle is one of the first big purchases you will make. If you need many vehicles to run your business, the costs can add up quickly. While these are one-time purchases, you also need to worry about maintenance costs, which become more frequent the longer it's been since you bought the vehicles. Don't forget about insurance too, including physical damage, bobtail insurance for trucks without trailers, and occupational accident insurance. While you might be tempted to go with cheaper insurance plans, this could result in a higher bill if an accident does occur.

Vehicle purchase and maintenance expenses are unavoidable, but good preparation will ensure these costs aren't a problem for you. Make budget estimates for new vehicles and maintenance, and set money aside for these expenses long before they appear. This way, you can deal with engine issues or flat tires quickly and without stress, helping your drivers get back on the road as soon as possible and minimizing delays.

Fuel

If you're driving thousands of miles, you're going to need to pay for thousands of miles of fuel. Unfortunately, fuel isn't cheap, so this can very quickly turn into tens of thousands of dollars of expenses. Fuel costs are less of a concern for businesses that service a local area, but they're still something you should keep in mind, no matter how far your vehicles drive on a daily basis.

If you have a good idea of how many miles you're going to cover, you can use this information to figure out how much money you should set aside for fuel costs. Take the miles per gallon of your vehicle and divide it by the cost of fuel per gallon, then multiply the result by your estimated mileage in a given length of time, and you will get an estimate of just how much you will spend on gas for the same length of time. If your business involves multiple trucks, make sure to account for all of them. Neglecting to consider fuel costs is a quick way to bankrupt yourself, but as long as you save enough money, you should be making enough in revenue to offset these costs.

Employee Wages

If your business employs other people, you'll need to make sure you account for their salaries in your expense estimates. Employee wages will hit your wallet harder as your business grows larger, but they shouldn't be ignored in smaller businesses either. Short of laying off employees or severely cutting workers' pay, there isn't too much you can do to minimize these expenses either. It helps to make sure you are only hiring the number of people that you need to do the amount of work you have. If business is slow, you may need fewer employees than you initially anticipated until things pick up, but don't under staff yourself either. If your business is seasonal, consider hiring employees on a seasonal basis as well.

Registering Your Company

Earlier, we talked about the importance of registering your company as an LLC. While the benefits are well worth the price, forming an LLC is still an expense you should account for when you're budgeting. You'll need to pay a state filing fee, the cost of which can vary by the state. If you completed the LLC process through a company with the help of an expert, you'll have to pay their fees as well. On top of this, you'll be expected to pay annual fees to keep your LLC current and valid. For the most part, these are unavoidable fees, but don't forget about them when you're calculating your expenses.

Taxes

Taxes are a significant expense for any business, and CDL businesses are just as heavily affected by them as any other. Whether you're running a business or having them taken out of every paycheck, "Taxes are your largest single expense" (Wheelwright, 2018, p. 20). Taxes take a cut of your business' profits, which can leave you with less money than you initially anticipated. However, while taxes are dreaded by just about everyone, do they really have to be so bad?

If you understand tax laws and follow the right steps, you can minimize the amount of money you pay out in taxes. When you make proper use of all available tax breaks, you can save yourself a lot of money, and a lot of stress too. We will discuss the specifics of lowering the amount you pay in taxes shortly, but for now, it is enough to know that no matter how much you end up paying, taxes should be factored into your expenses.

How to Maintain a Consistent Cash Flow

With so many expenses that could cost you thousands of dollars, you need to make sure you're generating and saving enough money to cover all of the costs that come with a CDL business. Part of this process is finding customers and making money from jobs, but another part is learning how to properly manage the money you make. If you spend the revenue from your first few jobs immediately, you're going to be completely caught off-guard when the bills come in, and you don't have any money saved up to pay them off. Without consistent cash flow and proper savings, the harsh truth is that your business won't last long. You need to keep your expenses low and keep your income high, as well as get into the habit of saving before spending.

Start Marketing

Marketing is the best way to find potential customers for your business. When you market yourself, you show others how your company does business and why they should choose you over your competitors. More customers means more revenue coming into your business, which can help to offset many of the costs generated from running a business. While marketing can add to your expenses at first, it is typically fairly cheap compared to the amount you'll be spending on trucks and fuel, and a great marketing strategy will more than make up for the amount you spend on it.

As your company services more customers, you're going to increase in size. This means your expenses will increase as well. To balance your income and spending, you'll want to have a solid, reliable financial plan that guides your purchasing habits and cuts down on wasteful spending.

Create a Financial Plan for Your Business

Your financial plan outlines all of the steps you need to take to become a profitable business and continue expanding your sales. Most contain multiple different components such as your sales forecast, your expenses budget, a statement of your current financial position, your cash flow projection, and an operations plan that explains your specific goals and how you plan to achieve them. Just like starting a business without long-term goals, trying to grow financially without a plan can leave you struggling to figure out what comes next and what you want to achieve. In a study of small business owners, results showed that "entrepreneurs who had a completed business plan for their venture were more than twice as likely to successfully grow their business as those who had no plan or an incomplete financial plan" (Wertz, n.d., para. 2). If you want to double your chances of success, a complete financial plan is mandatory.

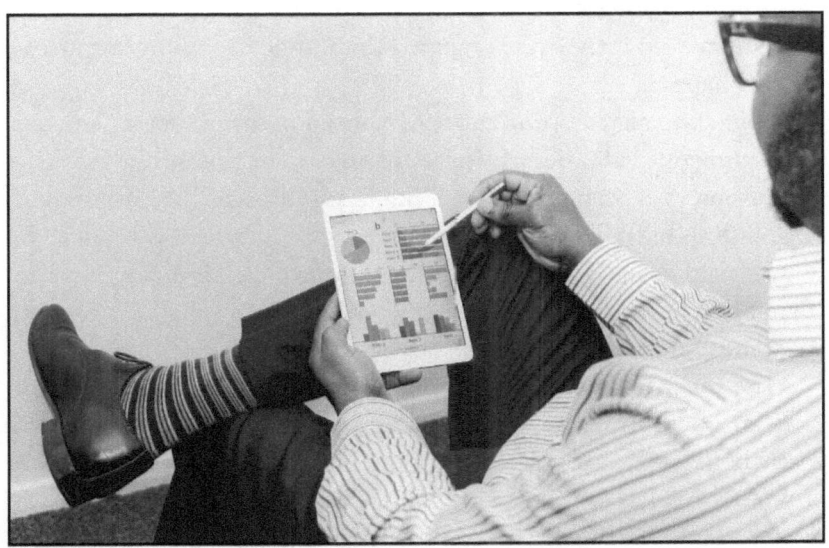

Begin with your sales forecast. This is an estimate of the revenue you will make from your sales. Try to make estimates on a monthly, quarterly, and yearly basis to paint a more complete picture. If you have previous sales, look back at these for your estimates and pay attention to any patterns that might arise—for example, certain types of businesses might do better seasonally or during certain kinds of weather. If you haven't been operating for a few months already, make a good estimate based on how many customers you have and how much you charge for your service. Getting a good idea of your current sales will help you figure out how much you want to grow your sales in the future.

Next, make a budget of all of your company expenses. We have already discussed the most common ones for CDL businesses, but include any others that are relevant to your company. Make sure you write down current operation costs and expected expenses you will have in the future. For example, if you want to grow your business, plan on spending more on the necessary expenses. You may also need to budget for wage increases or tax rate increases, as well as setting some money aside for unexpected expenses like damage to your business caused by fires or natural disasters. It's better to save money for these costs even if they don't happen than to be caught by surprise if they do happen.

Your statement of your current financial position should list your assets and your liabilities. Account for all of your assets, like machinery, inventory, and property, and make sure you include all of your outstanding bills. This step gives you an idea of where you are right now. If your assets outweigh your liabilities, you're on the right track. If your liabilities are much higher, you may need to see where you can cut some costs and pay off some of your bills.

The cash flow projection is similar to your sales forecast, but it looks at how much you will have left on a monthly, quarterly, and yearly basis. It is your income minus your expenses for a given period of time. If you have cash left at the end of each period, you can put that money to good use such as expanding or investing in your business. If you're short on cash, making a cash flow projection helps you notice this issue before it can build into extreme debt.

Now that you understand where you currently are, you can start looking towards the future with your operations plan. This overview will help you understand "what roles are required to operate your business at various volumes of output, how much output or work each employee can handle, and the costs of each stage of your supply chain" (Wertz, n.d., para. 25). A good operations plan will help you identify where there is room to grow and how you should make financial decisions in the future. Give yourself clear, measurable goals to work towards in the future, like increasing revenue 10% or lowering expenses by $5,000.

Make Your Taxes Work for You

Taxes are a large part of your operating expenses, but they don't have to be overwhelming. There are many ways to get your taxes to work for you. The process involves taking advantage of tax breaks available for your business, thereby minimizing the amount you are required to pay.

As a small business owner, there are many tax breaks available to you that don't require you to take advantage of loopholes. In fact, the government actually wants you to take advantage of these tax breaks. As professional CPA Thomas Wheelwright notes in his book *Tax-Free Wealth: How to Build Massive Wealth by Permanently Lowering Your Taxes*, tax codes are written "as government incentives and economic stimulus to keep the wheels of the economy greased and moving," (Wheelwright, 2018, p. 8) so you're doing exactly what the government wants by making the most of every tax break you can.

Here are some tax deductions that may apply to your business:

- Gas
- Travel expenses that are covered by the company
- Office supplies
- Vehicle maintenance costs like new tires, parts, and other repairs
- CDL licensing fees
- CDL education classes

- Mileage deductions
- Business and renter's insurance
- Startup expenses
- Employee salaries and benefits
- Home office expenses
- Phone and internet
- Loan interest
- Legal, bookkeeping, and accounting service fees
- Depreciation of vehicles
- Charity donations

Avoid Legal Fines

It's also important to make sure your business is compliant with all relevant laws and codes. Neglecting to do so could leave you with a hefty fine. Important areas to pay attention to are licensing, zoning, environmental laws, city ordinances, and safety.

For licensing requirements, make sure you and your employees all have the proper CDL credentials for the job. You may also need to get one or more endorsements if you're working in specific areas like passenger transport or hazardous waste transport. Check the licensing laws in your state as well as federal laws for transporting goods and people across state lines.

Zoning laws can throw a real wrench in your business if you don't check them before you begin operating. Some states have restrictions on where you can and can't start certain types of businesses. You may need to move your business elsewhere if you live somewhere that doesn't allow for business operations or for the large trucks or buses that your CDL company uses.

As a company with the potential to increase greenhouse gas emissions, you will be subject to many environmental health laws created by the Environmental Protection Agency (EPA). These laws ensure that transportation companies are operating in a way that reduces their carbon footprint. While you may have to work to abide by these policies in your business, you can get some tax breaks for following them too. For example, as part of the Clean Diesel Program, "The EPA offers grants and rebates for projects that improve air quality by reducing harmful emissions from diesel engines" (Entrepreneur, 2016, para. 23). Making use of these rebates can help you lower your expenses.

Your town or city may have specific ordinances that your business needs to follow. These ordinances may be about hours of operation or other guidelines for all businesses in the area, or there may be specific ordinances for your CDL business. Check local laws and keep up with any new ordinances passed to ensure you are in compliance with them.

Finally, you should ensure that your business is operating as safely as possible. While there is always a chance for accidents to occur, you should be doing everything in your power to reduce that chance. Big accidents could leave people seriously hurt, not to mention the fines and bad press you would get. Managing safety concerns in your business will be addressed in greater detail in a future chapter.

Make Use of People, Tools, and Other Resources That Can Help

There are plenty of tools that can help you manage your company's financial plan. It's a good idea to invest in an accounting software or a budgeting program so you can keep all of your financial information in one place. These programs can help you stay on track and hit your profit targets by highlighting any areas where your spending is exceeding your income.

If you find that you need more help than that, you may want to hire someone to help you manage your finances. While you should always be in charge of the direction you want to take your business, it's not a bad idea to hire an accountant who is responsible for the details of your expenses. Accountants can break all of your financial information down into something that's easier to understand, letting you make informed decisions for your company. Accountants can also help manage your taxes and identify where you can make use of tax breaks. While hiring or contracting an accountant may cost you some money, you typically make much more back by following their advice, so it's a good investment for your business as you continue to grow.

Take a CDL-Minded Approach to Your Expenses

The financial side of any business can be overwhelming, but if you treat it the same way you treat your other goals, it becomes an easier issue to manage. Consider what you want to achieve, then break it down into smaller steps to get there. If you want to increase your revenue, find new customers through marketing or increase your rates. If you want to improve your profit-to-expenses ratio, find ways you can cut out unnecessary spending. Set financial goals that will help you grow your company and assist you in achieving your other long-term goals.

CHAPTER
5

The Road to Obtaining Unlimited Freedom

Running your own company has its perks, and many of those perks come in the form of greater professional and personal freedom. After all, becoming an entrepreneur isn't a job for everyone. If you're okay sitting at a desk working a nine-to-five every day, pulling long hours, and trying to manage a limited number of sick days, then you wouldn't be so interested in starting and running a CDL business. You most likely wanted a little more control in your life and some more flexibility in your schedule. In short, you wanted to experience unlimited freedom. But what does unlimited freedom really look like, and how will starting your own CDL business help you experience it?

In the CDL industry, freedom comes in many forms. Even truck drivers who are employed by CDL companies can generally experience more freedom in their jobs than people who have corporate positions. There is no rigid structure in a trucking job. Drivers get to experience the freedom of the open road, and where they stop, eat, and sleep is largely at their own discretion. What supervision does exist is limited, as drivers are often hundreds of miles away from their supervisors. Additionally, commercial driving is a lucrative industry, and even the drivers experience greater financial freedom than what's offered at many other companies. However, there are still some limitations to this kind of freedom. Truck drivers may have to spend time away from home, and working long shifts is often just part of the job. This could mean less time spent with family. If you want to experience real, unlimited freedom, running your own company where you call the shots, gives you the most control over your own life and how you want to live it.

What unlimited freedom means to you, as a CDL-Minded Entrepreneur, is having the freedom to live as you see fit and the control and shape your life in the direction you want. You can work at your own discretion and create a business that reflects your own values and principles. You won't have anyone standing over your shoulder as you work criticizing your efforts, because you're the boss. A successful business means you can even spend freely, no longer tied down by extensive budgeting just to be able to afford the basics. There will be obstacles in your path as you expand your business, but when you overcome them, you will experience freedom like you've never known it before.

How to Achieve Freedom

The good news is that you're already on the right path to achieving freedom. You've made the commitment to owning your own CDL business, which will help you find freedom in your career that carries over to your personal life. Part of developing more control over your life is expanding your business and striving towards your goals, which is what you have been learning to do this whole time.

The not-so-good news is that you will still face some roadblocks on your way to freedom. Ironically, some of these obstacles come from freedom itself. After all, if you're not used to having control over your schedule, you might be more tempted to procrastinate important work. Without a clear path ahead of you, you might not know where to go. These kinds of obstacles are especially harmful because they don't seem like problems at first, which means you might not address bad habits until they've become ingrained in your schedule. You can overcome these obstacles, but only if you learn to recognize them.

Obstacles to Achieving Freedom

Too much freedom, too quickly, can leave us scrambling to readjust. The "freedom adjustment" here is so great because we have never experienced so much freedom before, which can leave us uncertain how to handle it (G-Town, n.d., para. 4). Think of a kid going to college for the first time and using their newfound independence away from home to cut class and attend parties, but with even fewer restrictions. If you can't adjust to the amount of responsibility you need to take for your own actions, you won't get important work done and the company will suffer.

Financial issues and debt are also obstacles to achieving freedom. One way to protect yourself from its effects is to register as an LLC. This ensures you're not going to be held personally responsible for any debts or legal trouble your company faces, which might otherwise compromise your financial freedom.

By far the biggest obstacle to your freedom, more than any financial hiccups your company may experience or competition you may face, is your own mindset. The danger of the freedom adjustment exemplifies how you can get in your own way even when the road ahead should be clear. If you can continue focusing on your goals and maintaining self-discipline even when the only thing keeping you from straying from the path is yourself, you can safely make the adjustment to unlimited freedom.

How to Apply Unlimited Freedom

As you adjust to the new levels of freedom you experience as a CDL entrepreneur, you may be left uncertain as to how you can manage your excess time, money, and control over your life. This freedom is everything you've been working toward, but what will you do with it now that you have it?

As always, whenever you feel directionless or lost, return to your goals. These will point you in the right direction. Consider what goals you've set for the future of your business. Have you achieved all of these, or can you keep working towards them? Are there ways that you can continue to grow your business, or are there other life goals that you can focus on now that you have a better financial situation? Consider the family and community goals you set and keep shaping your life as you see fit. Set new goals that bring you closer to achieving your life's purpose, whatever it may be.

Make sure to push away the desire to procrastinate now that you're free to do what you want. While it's okay to spend some time on celebrating the goals you've achieved, you don't want to get complacent and give up on the rest of your long-term goals. Use the momentum from establishing your business and get everything running by looking for ways to keep growing and expanding your business. This will keep you motivated and reduce the risk of putting off your goals.

How to Get Your Business Working for You

As you continue to grow your business, you may find that you don't need to be quite as directly involved as you did when you were just entering the industry. Hiring more employees means there are more people to take on the jobs you previously had to handle on your own. Outlining your goals and your plan to achieve these goals means you can just follow the steps you have already laid out for yourself. As you delegate tasks to others who become more confident and experienced in their roles over time, you won't need to work for your business—your business will start working for you, affording you much more free time and greater freedom overall.

You can continue to make money even while letting your company effectively run itself, by creating a good foundation and supervising your business' growth. With the right investments, your company will begin generating income like a well-oiled machine, all without you having to spend long nights at work and away from your family. The key to this lies in the three POIs and the three PORs of running your business. We will break these abbreviations down further shortly so you can see how each one applies to your business. They will allow you to take a more hands-off approach to your business, though you will still be the one responsible for guiding the direction of your company's growth and making all the big decisions.

The Overall Mindset Approach

While freedom is desirable, a great deal of freedom all at once can be hard to handle, especially if you're used to heavily structured jobs. If you maintain a good mindset and you don't lose focus, you can keep working towards bigger and better things. It's easy to get distracted by how much freedom you have, or to let concerns fall by the wayside. Resist the temptation and keep up the good work in all areas of your life. If you can continue to motivate yourself using your long-term goals and the lifestyle habits of routines, discipline, and focus, you can use your newfound freedom to achieve even more in life.

The Three POIs You MUST Know in Business

There are three different POIs you need to know in business. Each of these abbreviations will help you keep your business running profitably and allow you to generate cash flow with minimal effort. Putting them to good use can drastically improve your business' revenue, helping you build a business that works for you.

The three POIs are profit of investing, power of input, and producing ongoing income.

Profit of Investing

A great investment will pay out in dividends. When you invest, you give a little bit of your money, time, or other resources, and in exchange, you get an incredible return on your investment. A smart investment is always worth the initial cost. Just as you might invest in stocks, you can also invest in yourself and your company, with more reliable and predictable results than most stock traders enjoy. Through the profit of investing, you can make a small sacrifice work to your advantage.

The Law of Sacrifice was popularized by public speaker and life coach Bob Proctor, who identified it as "giving up something of a lower nature to receive something of a higher nature" (Proctor, 2011). It doesn't mean giving up important things like your health or massive amounts of money. Instead, it means letting go of something small to get something much better in return. Rather than being the painful experience you might associate with the word sacrifice, this law helps you achieve much more than you had before. This law shows us how working hard to overcome adversity can pay off for us, if we invest our time and energy appropriately.

Proper sacrifice is all about self-discipline. It is understanding that a little hardship now is worth the results you will see later. Your efforts are a small price to pay for the rewards you will reap. While investments are most commonly associated with finances, money isn't the only thing you can invest. You can also invest your time and energy to see really amazing results.

The most important places to make investments in are yourself, your family and your business. Investing in yourself involves cultivating skills like the lifestyle habits of discipline and focus. It means learning more about your business and understanding how you can continue to grow as a person and as a leader. Just by reading this book, you are investing in your future success. Investing in your business might involve paying for marketing campaigns to generate more business, hiring accountants for better financial health, or getting more trucks and drivers so you can keep up with demand. All these investments increase the future health of your business. Even if you have to pay a little money or spend more time outlining goals and plans now, the future success will more than make up for it.

Invest in people, tools, and other resources for your business as well. Offer training to your employees, so they can do their jobs more effectively. Invest in more expensive but higher quality vehicles to reduce the risk of drivers breaking down on the side of the road, which can lead to huge delays. When you work on improving what matters most, you will set yourself up to continue to succeed.

Power of Input

What you put into your business is what you get out of it. If you don't get the ball rolling, you'll never start your business at all. If you establish your business but you don't encourage its continued growth, you're not going to see the same results as someone who is constantly looking for ways to improve their business. The power of input highlights just how important it is to put in work so you can reap the rewards of that work later on.

Of course, it's also important to remember that not all ideas are necessarily good ones. If you try to expand your business too rapidly, you could end up bankrupting yourself from all the expenses before you ever get a chance to make back your money. Bad ideas can be just as dangerous as having no ideas for growth at all. It is up to you to evaluate ideas before you apply them in your business.

As the owner of your CDL business, your input and your ability to evaluate others' input is critical to your company's well-being. You may have many employees and advisors, but at the end of the day, it should be your vision that guides the company. If an idea doesn't align with your company's mission statement and it doesn't help you achieve your life's purpose, it may not be a good idea to incorporate it into your business plan. Carefully evaluate each decision and make sure it is the right one for your company.

When you get good input, act on it. Great advice is only useful if you actually put it into action. While you should take time to seriously consider big decisions, don't wait so long that the input is useless. Put your objectives and plans into action by embracing the new strategy.

Just like many other aspects of your business, the power of input starts with your mindset. Your long-term goals will play a large role in helping you decide what paths to follow and what advice could spell trouble for your company. If you are committed to growing your company and seeing your vision fulfilled, it will be much easier to put good input into practice.

Providing Ongoing Income

Your investments and good judgment allow your business to maintain a healthy cash flow. Your company can provide ongoing passive income, which is revenue that is acquired without direct work and accumulates on its own. It will continue to generate this passive income, and all you have to do to ensure continued cash flow is keep providing guidance. This is the stage where your earlier investments pay off.

There are many ways that you can increase the amount of ongoing income generated by your business. Most of these methods focus on increasing the number of customers your business serves, as this will allow you to continually increase your income without additional work on your part. Networking and looking for opportunities to collaborate with other businesses and business leaders can help you expand your customer base. So can making an effort to attend events related to your industry. Marketing is great for attracting new customers and increasing your revenue. You might also encourage your employees to follow up with leads and upsell current clients to make sure you're making as much money as possible out of each job. These are little ways to make a big difference in your ongoing income.

Making financial investments in stocks with your revenue is another way to generate passive interest. If you want to do this, it's a good idea to enlist the help of a trained professional, like a broker, to help you make good decisions, especially if you've never tried to invest before. You can make interest on your investment, and you can be paid dividends just by owning shares in certain companies. If your investment increases in value, the resulting income is known as capital gains. Investing can allow you to take advantage of certain tax breaks too. For example, "Passive income can be written off with passive losses, which are usually expenses associated with operating the income-generating activities" (Cussen, 2020, para. 22). These kinds of tax breaks will save you a lot of money, so they're worth the investment.

As you continue to grow your company, the amount of work you have to do will decrease over time. Your investments will generate their own income, and you won't have to spend all your time operating the minute details of the company. Your money works for you, not the other way around. This gives you the freedom to spend your time pursuing your other life goals.

Mastering the Three POIs for Power, Security, and Freedom

Learning and implementing the three POIs in how you run your business will bring you major financial success. These skills are crucial, and making good use of them will bring you closer to your long-term goals.

Each of the POIs can give you greater power over your life, greater security in your investments, and greater freedom overall. The profit of investing shows you how you can achieve more with your company through initial sacrifice that leads to future success. When you start investing, whether you invest in your own company or you invest your money in stocks, you will benefit greatly at the expense of only a relatively minor setback or financial contribution. These investments are worth what you get back.

You can further increase your chances of making good investments when you exercise good judgment with the power of input. The power of input helps you control where your company is headed so you can profit from its continued success. When all of the POIs are used together, financial concerns and wasted time and energy will be a thing of the past. With these key strategies, unlimited freedom is within your grasp, especially when you combine them with the three PORs.

The Three PORs You MUST Know in Business

The three PORs are all about setting goals for your company and maintaining a goal-oriented mindset. These abbreviations keep your focus on making future plans for your business that will help it continue to succeed. They emphasize the importance of being CDL-Minded and leveraging your time properly, choosing to spend your energy on the tasks that will actually help you achieve your goals. Through proper prioritization, you can ensure that you're not wasting energy on tasks that won't make a big difference on your level of success.

The three PORs are the power of reset, the profit of return, and the plan of reorganization.

Power of Reset

The power of reset is about rest and regeneration. When you are focused on your goals, it's easy to lose yourself in your work. You don't want to exhaust yourself, as this can lead to lower quality work. Taking a moment to reset your thoughts can help you refocus on what you need to be doing.

However, this rest is not idle. Instead of just taking a vacation day and relaxing on a beach, you should aim to calm your thoughts so you can achieve greater concentration. Your goals should be at the forefront of your thoughts as you mentally reset yourself. Through the power of reset, you will regenerate, not just your mindset now, but also your goals and plans for the future.

Focus can come from many different sources, and what you find helpful might be different from what someone else uses to reset. A little bit of exercise can get your blood pumping and clear your head. Try going on a light walk when you feel yourself getting frustrated or overwhelmed, or do a couple of jumping jacks in your office. You might feel a little silly, but the results are worth the temporary embarrassment. Other great strategies include breathing exercises and meditation. These help clear your mind of stressful thoughts, allowing you to center yourself and focus on what really matters. Meditate on your goals and visualize what achieving them might feel like. This can give you the motivation and clarity of thought to start working productively again.

It's best to avoid rest activities like watching TV or playing video games in the middle of work. Instead of helping you achieve greater focus, these kinds of activities pull your attention elsewhere. They're perfectly fine things to do when you're relaxing after work, but they're better left at home if you want to make real progress towards your goals.

Profit of Return

The profit of return is a strategy for executing plans or tasks that will actually generate interest for yourself. It means not wasting your time on the small stuff that doesn't have a big enough impact on the health of your business. It is closely related to learning how to leverage your time to achieve the greatest results. You can remain busy all day, but if the tasks you're doing don't matter, you won't get any of the important work done. Avoid doing work that doesn't need your attention and focus on the things that are going to have a real, measurable impact on your company. Using your time and energy strategically will enable you to get much more work done each day.

To better understand which actions are valuable and which ones aren't, consider the return on investment (ROI) of each of the actions you take. Your ROI is a measure of how much gain you get from doing a certain task. To calculate the ROI, compare your initial investment in time or money to the results of what you invested. For example, say you make phone calls to your customers and renegotiate your contracts. You make 10% more revenue in contracts than you otherwise would have made that day, so if you typically generated $1,000 in a day you would have made $1,100. Your ROI is the extra 10% gain, or $100 you made that day. Was this really a productive use of your time? Could you have done other tasks that would have brought in far more than an extra $100? If so, then you need to consider how to maximize your energy efficiency by doing tasks that have a bigger impact on your business' success.

To improve your ROI, consider how you could either complete these tasks more efficiently or let someone else handle them. Instead, you might choose to write out a single email and send it out to all of your previous customers, cutting down on the time investment, or you might delegate the task to someone else, as it doesn't require much expertise to do.

Delegation is a key skill for business owners to learn. Consider what each member of your team is best at and see if they would be a good fit for any of the tasks on your plate. This doesn't mean handing over anything you don't want to do; instead, it means analyzing your staff's strengths and weaknesses, and giving them the work they can complete more efficiently than anyone else.

Pass down tasks that take a lot of time and don't provide a great deal of value to your business. While these tasks may be necessary, they don't necessarily have to get done by you. For example, cleaning the bathrooms in the office is a necessary task that has to get done, but it would be unusual, to say the least, if you spent your energy scrubbing toilets instead of making important decisions for your business. Treat these busy work tasks the same way. Hand them off to other people so you can do the work that only you are capable of.

Delegating helps you avoid the trap of multitasking. While you're going to have many different responsibilities at any given time, trying to constantly switch your focus between each task is exhausting and a poor use of your energy. Rather than getting multiple tasks done in less time, "studies show that people are most productive when they focus on doing just one thing" (Santomassimo, n.d., para. 2). When you pick up different tasks, your brain undergoes a brief adjustment period. Think about how hard it would be to answer history and math questions at the same time on an exam—as your brain struggles to shift gears, you lose your focus and sacrifice your productivity. Trying to take on two different tasks at once can set you back in the same way. You'll get better results, and you'll work more efficiently, if you finish one task before moving on to another.

One more way to make sure you're using your time wisely is to pay attention to how much time you're spending on customers. It might be worth the extra effort to make sure your company lands a high-paying customer who will generate a lot of business, but if you're spending multiple days negotiating with customers who contribute very little to your business, you're spending a lot of time on something that doesn't provide much benefit. If you can, pass some of these lower-paying customers off to other employees who have been trained to handle customer service. This frees you up to focus on the customers who will make or break your business.

Plan of Reorganization

The plan of reorganization is the act or process of restructuring a current, new or pre-existing plan, to bring it to the next level. It is sometimes necessary to make changes to plans, once you start working towards your goals. You may find that your current strategy isn't getting you the results you want. Rather than continuing forward with a plan you know isn't working, it's better to stop, take a look at your plan, and see where you can make adjustments.

The plan of reorganization isn't just for plans that aren't performing as intended; it can also be used for plans you have already followed and used to achieve your goals. Once you hit your targets, keep pushing. Revisit your plan and see how you can increase your goals to bring you even greater success. Whether you have a faulty plan, an underperforming plan, or a successful plan that you have surpassed, reorganizing will help you create a new strategy to achieve more than what you initially planned.

Reorganization is critically important whether you're the owner of a CDL business or the President of the United States. One of the most well-known and effective uses of reorganization was the Reorganization Act of 1939, which was a congressional act carried out by Franklin D. Roosevelt around the time of the New Deal. The act allowed the president to "hire six assistants, propose reorganization plans subject to congressional veto, and make economy in government a priority," (Cengage, 2020, para. 2) and it eventually led to the establishment of the Executive Office. It was a big reorganization of the executive branch of the government. It allowed Roosevelt to enact many important policies that helped him pursue the vision he had for the nation, and it has done the same for generations of presidents after him. This reorganization was so important and so powerful that it is still in place today, affecting how our government is structured nearly 80 years later.

Of course, presidents aren't the only ones capable of reorganizing their plans. In finances, a reorganization plan is performed for businesses that have filed a chapter 11 bankruptcy. These plans describe "the process of how an insolvent company will change structurally to help it pay its debts and stay in business" (Farlex Financial Dictionary, 2012, para. 1). In order to pay off debts, things need to change in the business. Blindly continuing with the old plan of operation is exactly what led to bankruptcy in the first place. In order to mend the damage, reorganization and developing a new strategy is key.

You can make use of the valuable practice of reorganization long before you're facing potential bankruptcy. If a plan isn't working, or if it isn't working well enough, there's nothing wrong with changing it up and finding a new plan that better suits your needs. Shifting focus as soon as a problem becomes apparent will save you lots of wasted time and energy.

Mastering the Three PORs for Power, Security, and Freedom

Mastering the PORs is all about finding balance between them. For the power of reset, it's good to take a step back and refocus yourself on your goals, but spending too long thinking about what you're going to do can get in the way of actually doing it. When it comes to the profit of return, you want to cut out the unnecessary work in your schedule, but you still need to remain involved with your company to ensure it continues to grow. As for the plan of reorganization, this is a useful tool for fixing or expanding upon plans, but don't get caught in the planning stage forever. Remember to also take action once you've optimized your plan to the best of your ability; you can always make adjustments later on.

If you can find a comfortable balance with all three PORs, you will be right in the sweet spot that affords you the greatest power, security, and freedom in your business.

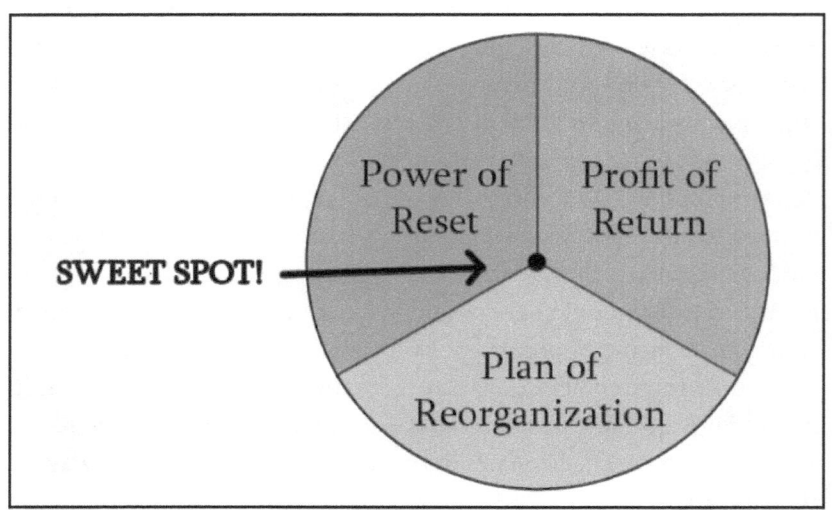

Additionally, pay attention to the way the three PORs tie into each other. Each POR creates a feedback loop with the others. The power of reset helps you clear your mind and focus your thoughts on your goals. Once you've done that, it is easier to make use of the plan of reorganization. Your goals are already in the forefront of your mind, so it's easier to see how you can restructure your plan to achieve them. When you've laid out your plan, use the profit of return strategy to make sure you're delegating each task in your plan appropriately. When you are only working on the tasks that provide the most benefit for your business, you are always focused on your big goals, which makes it even easier to use the power of reset. Each of the PORs leads into the next, creating a feedback loop that results in greater productivity and greater success.

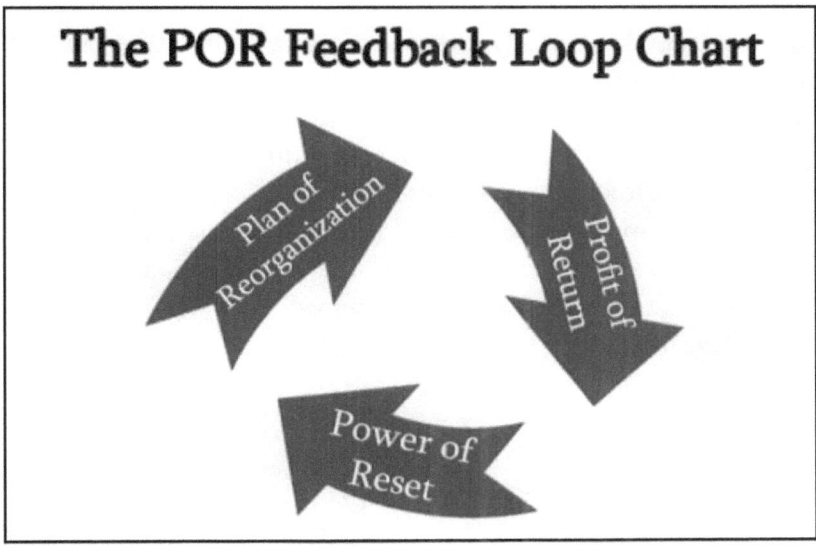

The POR Feedback Loop Chart

Plan of Reorganization

Profit of Return

Power of Reset

It is crucial to know, understand, and apply these PORs in your business. When you do, you support your goal-oriented mindset, and you constantly bring yourself closer to your goals. Along with the three POIs, these strategies can help you achieve unlimited freedom in everything you do.

CHAPTER
6

Maximizing Security Now for the Long Run

You might not think of CDL jobs as being especially dangerous, but many of them are actually full of potential security concerns. When you're driving around with hundreds or thousands of dollars' worth of goods in the back of your truck, it is no surprise that this poses a security risk. Other risks that can occur on the job are often related to long nights spent on the road, where exhausted drivers could pose a safety risk to themselves and others. There are also potential safety concerns for drivers that have to sleep in roadside motels or, worse, in their trucks when there aren't any motels with truck parking in sight.

As the owner of a CDL company, it is your responsibility to make sure both the driver and the goods arrive at their destination safely. Security concerns can lead to lost profits, lost customers, and even a shortage of employees. If drivers perceive their job as unsafe, they're less likely to stick with it. Take steps early to ensure your company is operating as safely as possible so you have these systems in place for the long run.

But what can you do to limit these security concerns and make sure your business is as safe as possible? Handling the issues begins with understanding the unique security threats posed to truck drivers and others in the CDL industry.

The Security Crisis in the CDL Trucking Industry

Trucking is the backbone of delivery services. Without truckers and others in the CDL industry, it would be impossible to ship things across the country for the low rates we currently enjoy. Despite this, there is a shortage of CDL-certified drivers that only worsens each year. Current estimates suggest that in the US alone, driver shortages are nearing 60,000 truckers, and "within the next eight years the shortage is predicted to reach a staggering 174,000" (Braw, 2018, para. 2). These driver shortages are partially a result of people perceiving the job as unsafe, which may discourage them from getting their CDL license.

Without new hires, security concerns only grow, creating a real security crisis. Here are a few of the biggest security issues in the CDL industry today.

Exhaustion

With fewer drivers in the industry than what is needed, the drivers who do work are often asked to work longer shifts later into the night. Driver exhaustion is a huge safety risk for any CDL company. The large size of most trucks means that a brief lapse of attention could lead to serious injury or even a deadly accident. Longer drives, especially those that are overnight, can seriously jeopardize your employees' safety.

Another side effect of the employee shortage are improperly trained employees. If drivers don't get the training they need to operate their vehicles safely, including going through any additional licensing procedures, they could be unfamiliar with their job duties and make more mistakes, especially if they are overworked. The consequences of these mistakes can range from relatively benign to very dangerous.

Expensive Cargo

If you're shipping expensive cargo, you're going to have concerns over its safety. This could mean shipping a few pricey things, or it could mean packing a truck full of less expensive items that add up to be worth much more. The more your cargo is worth, the greater the risk of it potentially getting stolen. An attempted theft could put your drivers at risk too depending on what they are shipping. Securing your cargo and reducing the risk of theft helps your employees feel safe.

Theft and Fraud

Just as theft can occur from outside the company, so too can it occur within the company. While you may want to think the best of your employees, the unfortunate truth is that some fraud is committed by people who work for the company they're stealing from. This kind of theft can be hard to police in the CDL industry, as drivers spend days at a time alone with just the cargo. One way to counteract it is to keep strict logs of what was shipped out and what arrived at its destination so you can spot any missing cargo right away. Keeping a close eye on your finances is another good way to reduce the chances of theft, and proper security training for all employees can limit the risk of fraud.

How to Overcome Liability and Work With Your Assets

Knowing the possible sources of security issues is only half the battle. The other half comes in the form of reducing the risk of security crises that negatively impact your business. Some solutions deal with recouping losses after an accident or theft has occurred, while others address the underlying issues that cause or allow for accidents and theft in the first place.

One method for reducing liability for accidents is buying insurance. This helps protect you from financial losses due to on-the-job accidents or destruction of company property. It can help you recover your losses, so they don't interfere with the health of your business. However, insurance only helps once a breach of security has occurred. While it's still a good idea, you should also look into ways to protect your cargo and your drivers before any theft or accidents have the chance to happen by lowering the chances of these safety hazards.

TWIC Cards

An increase in security concerns has led to the usage of Transportation Worker Identification Credential (TWIC) cards, which are typically required for drivers that come into contact with port facilities. TWIC cards "contain biometric information (human characteristics such as fingerprints) on a microchip, a magnetic strip, and a bar code, and require special reading devices for clearance and verification," (TruckingTruth, 2017, para. 5) and cardholders must also undergo a background check. While these security measures are extensive, they help to ensure the right people are getting access to secure facilities, and they limit the risk of fraud. Most over the road (OTR) drivers should get TWIC cards, so they can make and pick up shipments from secure maritime facilities. TWIC cards can also provide verified identification for these drivers at other locations.

Specific CDL Licenses and Endorsements

You must ensure that all of your drivers have the proper CDL licenses and endorsements for their jobs. Without them, they may lack the proper training and certification for the work they're doing. This can increase the risk of accidents and also increase your liability if an accident does occur.

The three different types of CDL licenses are categorized as Class A, Class B, and Class C. Each one allows license holders to perform different operations, and the training for each type of license is a little different.

Class A licenses are for combination vehicles like tractor-trailers. License holders can operate "any combination of vehicles that have a Gross Combination Weight Rating (GCWR) of 26,001 pounds or more," including towed units "with a gross vehicle weight of over 10,000 pounds" (Winnesota, 2018, para. 21). Class B licenses are for single vehicles of the same measurements, and Class C licenses allow for the operation of smaller vehicles with specialized purposes. These purposes include transporting 16 or more people or transporting hazardous waste.

On top of the different licenses, make sure your drivers have all necessary endorsements. These are necessary for certain jobs that are bigger safety hazards, and they typically require additional security screenings and a background check.

Applying Security in Your Business, Job, and Company

Safety and security should be a priority for your company. You should work to minimize the risk of workplace accidents wherever possible, and you should also limit the chances for theft or fraud to occur. Taking precautions early and following all safety guidelines will save you a lot of trouble in the long run.

If you maximize your security now, even if you only have a handful of employees, you won't have to worry about it as your business grows. You can maintain the same safety regulations and just scale them up to account for your business' growth. Take security measures seriously from day one to protect your assets so you don't end up a victim of theft. When you apply security in all aspects of your business, you protect yourself from future losses.

Overall Mindset Approach

Security concerns interfere with your long-term goals. Every security breach sets you back from where you want to be on your path to success. Every exhausted employee makes it harder to stick to the mission and vision statements you made when you founded your company. Security should be a key part of your mindset and your goals if you want to continue working towards your life's purpose.

Manage safety concerns as soon as they appear, and work to minimize security risks before they can become a problem. If you maintain a safe working atmosphere, it will be much easier to focus on achieving your overarching goals. Reduce your risk of liability for accidents, not just by protecting yourself legally and financially with insurance but also by reducing the risk of accidents. This makes your business a safer place to work, builds trust with your employees, and helps you reduce potential obstacles in order to achieve unlimited freedom as a CDL business owner and entrepreneur.

STEP 3

Living the CDL-Minded Lifestyle

CHAPTER 7

The Value of Balancing Work, Family, and Play in Your Life

Our culture tends to praise workaholics. We correlate success with hard work, which means that if we want to be successful, we believe we have to spend every waking moment working for that success. However, is this really true, or is the celebration of the workaholic actually doing more harm than good?

To be sure, there must be hard work in every success. You're not going to launch your own CDL business without facing some challenges and putting in the effort to overcome them. Still, focusing on work to the exclusion of all other aspects of your life isn't healthy, and it's not as fulfilling as living a well-balanced life. In fact, rather than reducing your productivity, taking some time to relax can actually help you be more productive when you're working. We need to have downtime in our lives, and we need to walk the careful tightrope that is work-life balance.

Our lives should be full of work, family, and play, not just one or two of these aspects. Each contributes to a positive, healthy mindset, and learning to balance them all successfully keeps us productive and fulfilled.

The Importance of Work, Family, and Play

Work, family, and play are all necessary components of a happy and satisfying life. If you work until you feel ready to drop, you never get the chance to enjoy the fruits of your labor, and you can burn out quickly. If you focus only on living for your family, you might put personal and career goals aside, even if you still desire those goals. If you only ever play, you miss out on all the other experiences life has to offer through work and family. Each aspect is important to our lives, and each one plays a key role in keeping us well-rounded.

Some people see work as just something that pays the bills, and in many industries and jobs, that tends to be the case when it comes to work. However, when you run your own CDL company, work becomes much more than that. It is a way to achieve financial freedom, but it is also a way for us to feel a sense of purpose in our lives. It gives us a way to direct our efforts and make progress towards our life's purpose. Remember that work isn't limited to just our jobs. It can also encompass personal projects we take on and any volunteer work we do for others. When we feel like we are making a positive difference with our work, we experience the greatest levels of professional and personal satisfaction.

Spending time with our families is equally important to our well-being. Too much work can interfere with your personal life, which can keep you from seeing your family as often as you would like. You might miss important milestones and parties, which can strain your personal relationships. When we share time with our families, we grow closer as a family unit, and we reinforce our motivation for working. We start to see success not just as something that benefits us but also as something that benefits our families.

Play is often perceived as less important than work or family time, but it is actually crucial to our mental and emotional health. Hobbies and other fun activities engage us outside of work. They give us a way to de-stress at the end of the day and take our minds off of our work. Spending leisure time with friends also helps us feel more connected to them and fulfills our need for socialization. Group activities like playing a board game or video game together, going on a walk or hike, and practicing hobbies together are all great ways to share our recreational time with others.

When we take some time away from work to play or spend time with our families, we get to enjoy what all of our efforts have brought us. Work seems more purposeful because we know what it's helping us to achieve. Play and family time reinforces our goals, and we put these goals into motion at work. We are more motivated and it is easier to continue striving towards success.

Working Smarter, Not Harder

Spending too much time at work can reduce the amount of time you have available for family and leisure time. When you have a lot of things you need to get done and not much time to do them in, how do you manage all of your responsibilities? The solution is learning to work smarter, not harder. We've already discussed time management and how to leverage your time effectively, but there are many more solutions you can use to reduce your workload just by changing the way you work. You can get the same amount of work done in a fraction of the time and energy you would otherwise spend on it with these habits and tricks. This frees up your schedule and fixes your work-life balance without allowing any important tasks to fall by the wayside.

Invite Feedback

Feedback often uncovers the bad and negative habits that cause us to work hard instead of working smart. Other people are usually much better at pointing out our flaws than we are, and they can identify areas where we're wasting time and working inefficiently. Look for feedback on any task you have difficulty with, especially if you can ask a mentor or expert in the area. Even if you think you're great at something, you can almost always improve, and these improvements will save you a lot of time and effort.

The best feedback is specific and actionable. Remember that just because someone is an expert in their field, this doesn't mean they're an expert at giving advice. Some of the burden falls on you to ask the right questions. Point out specific parts of the task that are difficult for you and ask questions not just about what's wrong but how you can improve. When you improve the quality of your work (and learn a few tips from experts while you're at it), you won't have to spend nearly as long workshopping and revisiting tasks. If you have the time to fix something, it takes even less time to get it right on the first try.

Practice Being Concise

A lot more time is wasted in being long-winded than you might think. If you sit and stew over the best way to write a one-line email, you've turned a 10-minute task into a half-hour-long one. If you're speaking to a customer and you waste time explaining a ton of information that doesn't matter for the sale, you can double the time you spend meeting with people, not to mention making it harder for them to pay attention to the part of your speech that's actually relevant to them.

Being concise helps you get your point across clearer, which minimizes confusion. When you are brief and blunt where appropriate, it's easier for others to understand what you're saying and follow your directions. You don't need to be so brief you come off as rude, but you don't need to go running to the thesaurus every time you write a memo either. While million-dollar words might make you sound smarter on the surface, they can get in the way of getting your message across. Why say "fallacious" when you could simply say "wrong"? People will know what you are saying, which makes you a more efficient communicator.

Keep Learning

There is always so much more to learn, both as a business owner and as a person. The more you learn, the more you can apply your new knowledge to your work. Becoming an expert in your field helps you keep your business competitive, and it helps you narrow down your focus to the work that matters.

When you stop learning, you limit your potential for growth. You spend just as long on tasks after years of practice as you did when you first started doing them. You waste time making improvements in areas of your business that won't help you attract more customers. Learning is what keeps your head above water as a business owner. Continue developing your skills and trying to improve your efficiency every day. Learn to do things the easy way and you'll save yourself a lot of hassle.

Avoid Overworking Yourself

You can't work hard all the time. If you do, you will only burn out quickly. Your work quality will suffer, you'll feel unmotivated to finish even small tasks, and you'll have a hard time really caring about what you're doing. If you convince yourself that the only way to achieve your goals is to work hard all the time without any breaks, achieving your goals won't sound so desirable after all.

Take breaks when you need them throughout the workday. If you finish a difficult task, give yourself five or 10 minutes to rest before jumping into the next thing. Avoid bringing work home with you, physically or mentally. If you get home and you find you're still thinking about work, you're effectively still in "work mode" which makes it impossible to actually relax. You need to find time for leisure and time for family in your schedule or you put your motivation at risk.

Find Time to Relax With Your Family

It can be hard to organize shared family time. Kids have school, clubs, sports, hobbies, and time spent with their friends. Your spouse likely has a job and hobbies of their own. Other relatives like parents and siblings may have busy schedules too. Despite these difficulties, it is still crucial to spend time with your family and make lasting memories with each other.

Family time is more than just sitting and watching TV together. Strive for shared experiences that bring your family together and reinforce the values you want to teach your kids. This could mean playing a game, doing an activity together like cooking or camping, having open and honest conversations, or even just finding the time to have dinner together.

Why Family Time Matters

One of the most important benefits of family time is also one of the most straightforward. When you are more present in your family, you reinforce the family bonds. If you're never around, it's easy to feel like the family is destabilized. Long nights at work mean you're missing from a lot of important life events. Just making an effort to leave work on time shows your family you care about them and brings you closer together.

Shared family experiences can also help teach kids important lessons. Kids learn a lot of their early behaviors from their surroundings, and their parents in particular. If you want to teach them good behaviors, spending time with them is the best way to do so. More family time can help kids foster a positive mindset, improve their academic grades, and much more. They will build important skills that they will put into practice their whole lives.

Finally, family time reminds you what you are working for. Money isn't just a tool to have an easier life. It's also a way to give the people you love a better life. It's a way for you to provide for them and make sure their lives are as happy and fulfilling as your own. This can motivate you to work even harder as you remind yourself why your work matters.

Make Time for Recreation

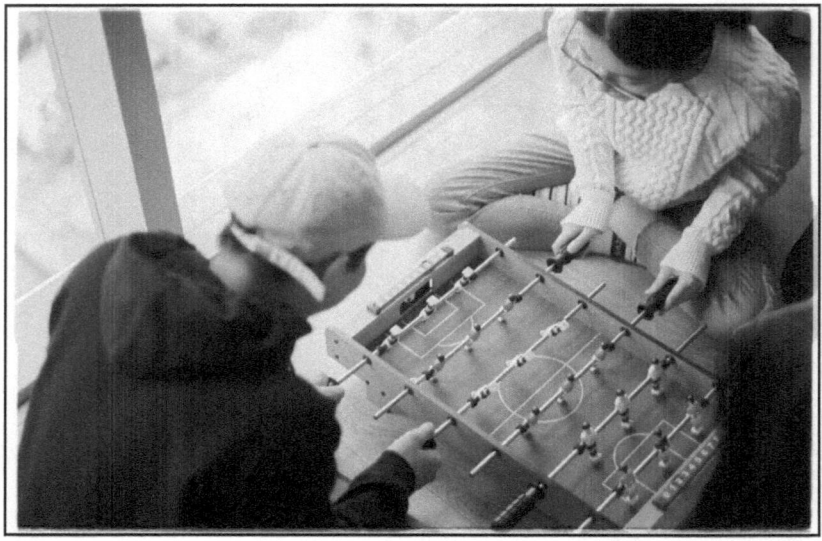

Play doesn't have to end just because you're an adult. In fact, it's actually good for adults to continue to seek out opportunities for recreation in their lives. Recreation functions as stress relief and helps take your mind off of difficulties you may be facing at work or in other areas of your life. It gives you a way to cope with difficult emotions and puts you in a more positive state of mind. When you take some time for leisure, you can return to work refreshed and ready to go. Playing also helps you get the creative juices flowing, which can improve your decision-making at work.

One of the easiest ways to fit more fun into your life is to add it to your schedule like you do work. This might not be the most spontaneous way to play, but it ensures that you'll take playtime as seriously as you do working hours. Doing something fun each day is just as important for your productivity as setting aside time to focus on work, so you should treat it with the same weight on your schedule.

If you're running low on time, try making other activities (that you need to get done) more fun. For example, if you exercise every day, choose an exercise you enjoy and that feels more like play than work, or get your daily fitness goals in by playing a sport. Make work a little more fun by introducing events like pizza parties and team-building activities. See where you can make your time at work a little more lively and make a conscious effort to have a little more fun every day.

Overall Lifestyle Approach

A good balance of work and leisure will make you much more productive in the long run. You will have an easier time achieving your goals, and when you are well-rested, you will come into work with a clearer head, ready to tackle whatever the day throws at you. Take every opportunity to remind yourself why your work matters and what it helps you achieve, whether this means carving out family time or enjoying your newfound free time.

Instead of living a life that is all work and no play, turn work into play. You can cut down on harmful habits like procrastination by making tasks more fun. Pure and simple fun is an amazing motivator. Take the example of the piano stairs that were installed in a subway station which were engineered so "as people climbed up the stairs, each step would play a different musical note" (Fabrega, 2013, para. 8). Even this tiny change encouraged more people to take the stairs, a task which they might otherwise have avoided. Make unpleasant tasks just a little more fun and you'll finish them faster and with a better mindset, embracing both work and play into your life.

CHAPTER 8

Embrace Constant Change

"The only thing constant is change"
—Heraclitus of Ephesus

Change is inevitable. No matter how much experience you have or how evergreen your niche, you will experience change in some form or another. Some businesses try to stick with what they know, failing to accommodate the change and losing business as a result. Others will try to keep up with new development but won't know how to stay relevant in an ever-changing marketplace. Understanding trends in your market and adapting to change as it happens is the only way to ensure that your business continues to thrive for years to come.

If you don't change with the times, the world will leave you behind. Embracing change is mandatory for any business. Constant evolution and adaptation will help your business keep up with new developments and remain competitive. Rather than fighting against change, welcome it, as it represents a new opportunity to grow and expand your company.

Changes and Challenges in the CDL Industry

Being able to predict changes in your market keeps you ahead of the curve. When you know change is coming, it is much easier to adjust your business strategy and your goals to match. We're not able to stop or reverse time, as much as we might want to. We can only affect how we react or respond to life's many inevitable changes.

While you can't predict the future, you can focus on certain aspects of the CDL industry that are constantly experiencing changes. Keep a close eye on new trends in these areas and consider how they might affect your business. Try to stay proactive in your responses to these trends so you aren't left behind when they occur.

Shifting Markets

A shifting market can make or break your company. Businesses that operate seasonally or only in certain weather conditions are at a greater risk of change than most, as business will fluctuate wildly throughout the year. If you're unprepared for these changes, they can leave you scrambling to break even on operating costs in the off-season.

Still, even the most reliable markets don't last forever. While commercial driving itself is a relatively stable industry—transporting goods through trucking has been around since the late 1800s and isn't likely to disappear—the more specific niches in each market may come and go. As a small business, you might focus on a single region or a certain transportation niche that could very well change in the next few years. It's best to watch for early warning signs of changes in your niche and react as early as possible.

Changes in Vehicles and Other Equipment

As years go by, vehicles break down and become outdated. The type of trucks, buses, vans, or shuttles you use now will probably not still be in use a decade into the future. The same is true for a lot of the other equipment your CDL business may use.

Upgrading to newer vehicles and equipment can be a costly expense, but it's a necessary one. Old vehicles can become unsafe over time and standards for equipment safety may change. Luckily, this change rarely occurs without plenty of warning. If you anticipate your vehicles becoming outdated and you save enough money ahead of time to replace your fleet, you shouldn't have too many difficulties adapting to this kind of change.

New Tax Laws and Regulations

Governments are constantly updating tax codes, many of which will affect you as a small business owner. Some of these changes will benefit you, giving you more opportunities for tax breaks. Others will saddle you with higher taxes which could become a big problem if you can't find ways to keep your business profitable. Thoroughly reviewing new tax laws will help you understand how the changes apply to you and how you can take advantage of any new tax breaks.

Legal regulations for CDL businesses may change over time as well. Pay attention to federal, state, and city laws regarding how and where your business can operate, and follow any new changes as quickly as possible. The fine you might receive for violating a regulation is much worse than the minor inconvenience of changing your operation strategy.

How to Manage Change

If change is going to happen whether you want it to or not, how do you learn to manage it? It's hard to transition your business to a new plan for operation, but if you don't, you put your company's success in jeopardy. Long-term success requires you to recognize, address, and respond to change effectively. The best ways to accomplish this is to start expecting change and to try to see change in a more positive light.

Learn to Expect Change

Change catches us off-guard if we don't learn to expect it. This can make it much harder to adjust to our new circumstances, especially if we grow too attached to our old ones. While we'll likely always feel some nostalgia for the early days of our businesses, we need to accept that our lives can turn on a dime. Something we take for granted today could be taken away from us tomorrow. This hurts most when we cling desperately to the past, but it's not so painful when we start to see it coming.

When you start expecting change to occur, you mentally prepare yourself for it. Keeping track of new trends isn't just a way to maximize your income. You adjust your mindset, which helps you see change as a promising opportunity rather than a burden.

See Change as an Opportunity

Change doesn't have to be a negative force in your life. Instead, it can represent a great new opportunity to expand your business into new markets, increase your profits, and try something new. It might disrupt your life a bit, but if nothing ever changed, life would be pretty boring.

Change gives you a chance to test the waters of new markets and try out different goals. It can be the encouragement you need to go out on a limb and attempt something you wouldn't have otherwise. You've already used change for this exact purpose. After all, becoming a CDL entrepreneur is a big change in your life, but it's a change that is well worth it. Your life wouldn't be the same if you had decided to reject change and allow the opportunity to run your own business pass you by. Embracing change can help you accomplish things that you never thought were possible.

Overall CDL-Minded Approach

Fear of the unknown is natural. It's completely normal to worry about potential changes in the market that could affect the way you run your business. Uncertainty and doubt are common when starting something new. However, these feelings don't have to hold you back if you don't let them. A little bit of fear is necessary for real, lasting change. It means you're trying something you've never done before that has the opportunity to turn your life around.

If you learn to anticipate and accept change, you will have a much easier time adjusting to it. Identify what changes you will need to make ahead of time. This will let you put yourself in a good position for adjusting to the change as smoothly and effectively as possible. With the right mindset and sufficient preparation, there is no change you can't overcome.

Conclusion

"A bad attitude is like a flat tire.
If you don't change it, you won't go anywhere."
—Joyce Meyer

As an entrepreneur and a CDL owner and operator, your mindset is your greatest advantage. The right mindset that focuses on setting and achieving goals that align with your life's purpose will get you wherever you want to go in life, whether it's starting your own CDL business or using the freedom from your company to continue accomplishing bigger and better things.

Throughout this book, you have learned the value that being CDL-Minded provides. You've learned how to set goals and how to use the GAME plan to follow through on your goals. You have a good understanding of what it takes to run a successful CDL small business, including managing your finances, leveraging your time, maintaining a good work-life balance, and embracing change wherever it appears in your life. You also know how your mindset can set you up for success and freedom in your career and in your personal life.

Now that you know exactly what it takes to run a CDL business, you are ready to start your own. As you create and expand your business, keep your thoughts on the future, but take action today. Success as a CDL entrepreneur and all of the benefits it affords are within your reach. You just need to get started.

If you have enjoyed this book and you feel it provides valuable information, consider leaving a review on Amazon. This helps more people find advice for starting their CDL business that really works and allows them to experience the same freedom that awaits you.

Special Bonus Offer: Free Gift for You! :)

Thank you! Here's a Free Gift! For You :)

As a special thanks from me to you, you'll receive:

- ❏ **3 Powerful Elements of Productivity in your Business**
- ❏ **5 Simple Strategies to Mastering Productivity in your Business**
- ❏ **The Highest Quality of Productivity Charts**
- ❏ **Valuable Resources that you Must Know and much more!**

To receive your Free copy of the CDL Business Productivity GAME PLAN, you can go to my website at:
cdlforlife.com/cdl-business-resources

<u>**SCAN ME**</u>
(For your Free Business Game Plan)

<u>**SCAN ME**</u>
(If you want my Books for Free)

Also If you would like to get my books for Free and before anyone else, go to my website at:
cdlforlife.com/cdl-business-resources

Appendix

Common Marketing Terminology

- Brand awareness: the extent to which people can recognize and remember your company
- Call to action: a request for a reader or listener to complete a certain action
- Digital marketing: marketing that occurs online
- Key performance indicator (KPI): any variable measured to show how well your business is performing in a certain area
- Market trends: changes in a specific industry or field over time
- Remarketing: reconnecting with people who have shown interest in or used your service before
- Return on investment (ROI): a measure for evaluating the effectiveness of a marketing strategy or other investment relative to its cost
- Word-of-mouth marketing: marketing that occurs through recommendation of your services from a satisfied customer to other potential customers

CDL Trade Publications

- Advanced Transportation Technology News
- American Shipper Magazine
- American Trucker
- Bulk Transporter
- Business Examiner

- Commercial Motor
- Fleet Executive
- Keep on Truckin' News
- Logistics & Transport Focus
- Modern Bulk Transporter
- Road King Magazine
- The Trucker
- World of Truckers

Trade Associations and Industry Events for Networking

- Accelerate! Conference and Expo
- American Trucking Association Management Conference & Exhibition
- CVSA Annual Conference and Exhibition
- CVTA Conference
- Mid-America Trucking Show
- National Association of Fleet Administration Annual Institute & Expo
- National Association of Small Trucking Companies
- Omnitracs Outlook
- The Work Truck Show
- TMC Annual

Templates

Trucking Business Plan Templates

- General Freight Trucking Business Plan (https://www. bplans.com/general_freight_trucking_business_plan/ executive_summary_fc.php)

- General Motor Freight Trucking Business Plan (https://www.bplans.com/general_motor_freight_trucking_business_plan/executive_summary_fc.php)
- Limousine Taxi Business Plan (https://www.bplans.com/limousine_taxi_business_plan/executive_summary_fc.php)
- Taxi Business Plan ((https://www.bplans.com/taxi_business_plan/executive_summary_fc.php)
- Truck Stop Business Plan (https://www.bplans.com/truck_stop_business_plan/executive_summary_fc.php)

Budget Calculation Templates

- Quickbooks: budget template (https://quickbooks.intuit.com/r/budgeting/essential-small-business-financial-tools-free-startup-budget-template-and-guide/)
- Smartsheet: marketing budget templates (https://www.smartsheet.com/12-free-marketing-budget-templates)

References

Beck, J. (n.d.). *Family standing on the beach*. Unsplash. https://unsplash.com/photos/a-nWU0o73r4

Blake, J. (2017, Mar. 13). *What is your happiness formula?* OWN. http://www.oprah.com/inspiration/jenny-blake-what-is-your-happiness-formula#ixzz5cypGE6w9

Braw, E. (2018, Sept. 19). *Trucking is the security crisis you never noticed*. Foreign Policy. https://foreignpolicy.com/2018/09/19/trucking-is-the-security-crisis-you-never-noticed/

Briscoe, J. (n.d.). *Checking stocks*. Unsplash. https://unsplash.com/photos/Gw_sFen8VhU

Carstens-Peters, G. (n.d.). *Writing a checklist*. Unsplash. https://unsplash.com/photos/RLw-UC03Gwc

Cengage. (2020, May 27). *Reorganization Act of 1939*. Encyclopedia.com. https://www.encyclopedia.com/economics/encyclopedias-almanacs-transcripts-and-maps/reorganization-act-1939

Crawford, R. (n.d.). *Wood truck on the road*. Unsplash. https://unsplash.com/photos/99HLgU4IHLY

Cussen, M. P. (2020, Jan. 30). *How will your investment make money?* Investopedia. https://www.investopedia.com/articles/financial-theory/09/how-investments-make-money-income.asp

DeLawrence, O. (n.d.). *Tax statements*. Unsplash. https://unsplash.com/photos/5616whx5NdQ

Entrepreneur. (2016, June 6). *The legal ABCs of running a transportation service*. https://www.entrepreneur.com/article/273812

Farlex Financial Dictionary. (2012). *Plan of reorganization*. https://financial-dictionary.thefreedictionary.com/Plan+of+Reorganization

Farrow, J. (n.d.). *Truck driving at dawn*. Unsplash. https://unsplash.com/photos/ucuOscdCaO4

Free-Photos. (2015, Sept. 7). *Sharpened pencil*. Pixabay. https://pixabay.com/photos/pencil-sharpener-notebook-paper-918449/

G-Town. (n.d.). *The freedom of trucking: Blessing or curse?* TruckingTruth. https://www.truckingtruth.com/trucking_blogs/Article-3898/the-freedom-of-trucking

Incorporate.com. (n.d.). *Start a trucking company in eight steps*. https://www.incorporate.com/learning-center/start-trucking-company-eight-steps/

Janssens, E. (n.d.). *Coffee and a monthly planner*. Unsplash. https://unsplash.com/photos/aQfhbxailCs

Kirb, L. (n.d.). *Asleep at the wheel*. Unsplash. https://unsplash.com/photos/5tniytQs68E

Langford, S. (n.d.). *Timex analog clock*. Unsplash. https://unsplash.com/photos/eIkbSc3SDtI

Meyes, D. (n.d.). *Rusted tow truck*. Unsplash. https://unsplash.com/photos/XZQacH1x1rE

Moran, J. (n.d.). *Man standing on a cliff*. Unsplash. https://unsplash.com/photos/hrEJYRtBDrk

Nizal, A. (n.d.). *Man running on the seashore*. Unsplash. https://unsplash.com/photos/L5Lt0e7Kjxc

Proctor, B. (2011, Nov. 6). *11 forgotten laws—The law of sacrifice* [Video]. YouTube. https://www.youtube.com/watch?v=NFienuvDsnY

Progressive Insurance. (n.d.). *Person looking at charts and graphs*. Unsplash. https://unsplash.com/photos/unRkg2jH1j0

Reyes, A. (n.d.). *Work flow chart*. Unsplash. https://unsplash.com/photos/qWwpHwip31M

Santomassimo, R. (n.d.). *3 steps to better utilizing your time for higher commissions*. The Massimo Group. https://massimo-group.com/time-utilization/

Shinn, F. S. (2005). *The Game of life and how to play it*. Florence Shinn.

Sincerely Media. (n.d.). *Glasses resting on a book*. Unsplash. https://unsplash.com/photos/c1YrcFYW66s

Souza, L. (n.d.). *Tour buses.* Unsplash. https://unsplash.com/photos/bAFWnhGAvxk

Tadyanehondo, N. (n.d.). *Aerial photo of freight trucks.* Unsplash. https://unsplash.com/photos/GOD2mDNujuU

Tantara. (2019, July 10). *Eleven reasons you should become a truck driver.* https://www.tantara.us/news/eleven-reasons-become-truck-driver/

TruckingTruth. (2017, Mar. 21). *TWIC cards.* https://www.truckingtruth.com/wiki/topic-45/twic-cards

Truong, B. (n.d.). *Man and woman playing foosball.* Unsplash. https://unsplash.com/photos/hYrnz92-bpY

Washington, D. (2017, Mar. 29). *Amazing motivational speech by Denzel Washington - Claim your dream 2017* [Video]. YouTube. https://www.youtube.com/watch?v=EBGb40yh4SY

Wicks, B. (n.d.). *Close-up photo of a watch.* Unsplash. https://unsplash.com/photos/kvzV9gHv1ic

Winnesota. (2018, Sept. 5). *CDL endorsements for commercial drivers: The ultimate guide.* https://www.winnesota.com/news/cdlendorsements

Ziglar, Z. (n.d.). *The Seven Steps of Goal Setting.* https://curvefinder.com/wp-content/uploads/2016/08/Goal-Setting-Canvas-1.pdf

Thank you for your Honest Experience :)

Thank you! I hope this brings you great value as it did for me sharing my story with you.

My purpose and mission is to guide and encourage you to become the best version of yourself in your life by providing everything you need to achieve your dreams for yourself, your family and your business.

However, in order to do that, sharing your honest review on **amazon** (or Audible) helps spread the word to other CDL Minded friends (like yourself) and will help many readers who are struggling to make their dreams become a reality.

If you do have 30 secs to leave a **1-Click honest review,** I greatly appreciate it because it shows that you're not like most people.

It means that you truly value yourself in what you do. It also means that you're CDL Minded in yourself, your family and in your business.

I truly appreciate all your love and support and I'm thankful and grateful for your life and I greatly value your honest opinion and thoughts. :)

If you need anything, feel free to reach out at my website and to receive your Free Gift if you haven't received it yet.

You can also share your experience by taking a photo of this book and attach it to the review so other CDL Minded friends can be inspired and encouraged from your honest experience.

SCAN ME!

Just One Click (once you click on this review page or scan QR Code):

When you finish, just Click Submit at the bottom of the page and that's it. Please click on this link or scan the QR code to **Review Book on Amazon!**

Overall rating
☆☆☆☆☆

Add a headline

    What's most important to know?

Add a photo or video
Shoppers find images and videos more helpful than text alone.

    +

Add a written review

    What did you like or dislike? What did you use this product for?

Submit

Looking forward to working together and helping you achieve your goals. Take care and talk to you soon! :)